DREAM BIG

COLORING BOOK

This book is dedicated to:

Amelia, Amber and Maisie

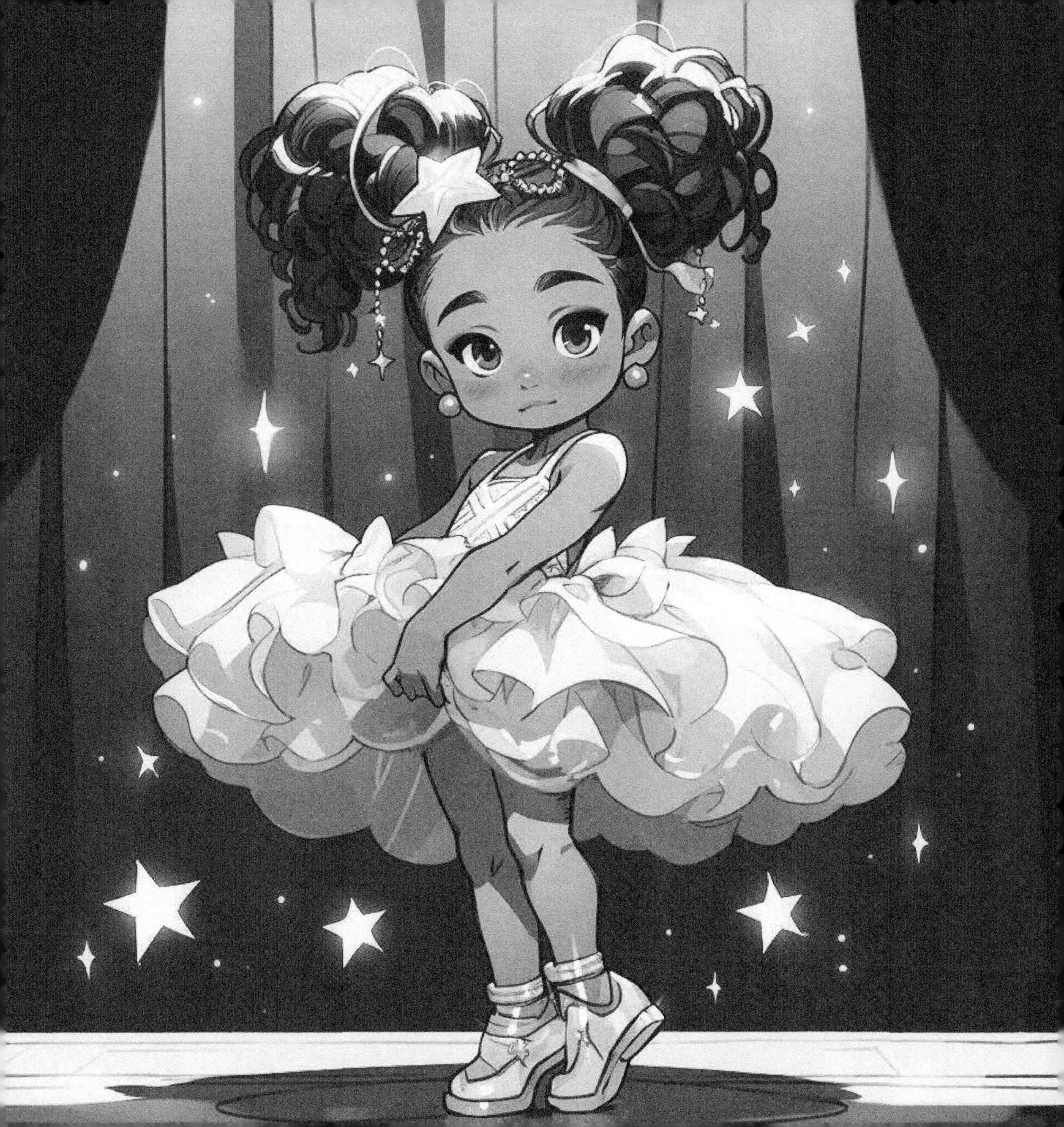

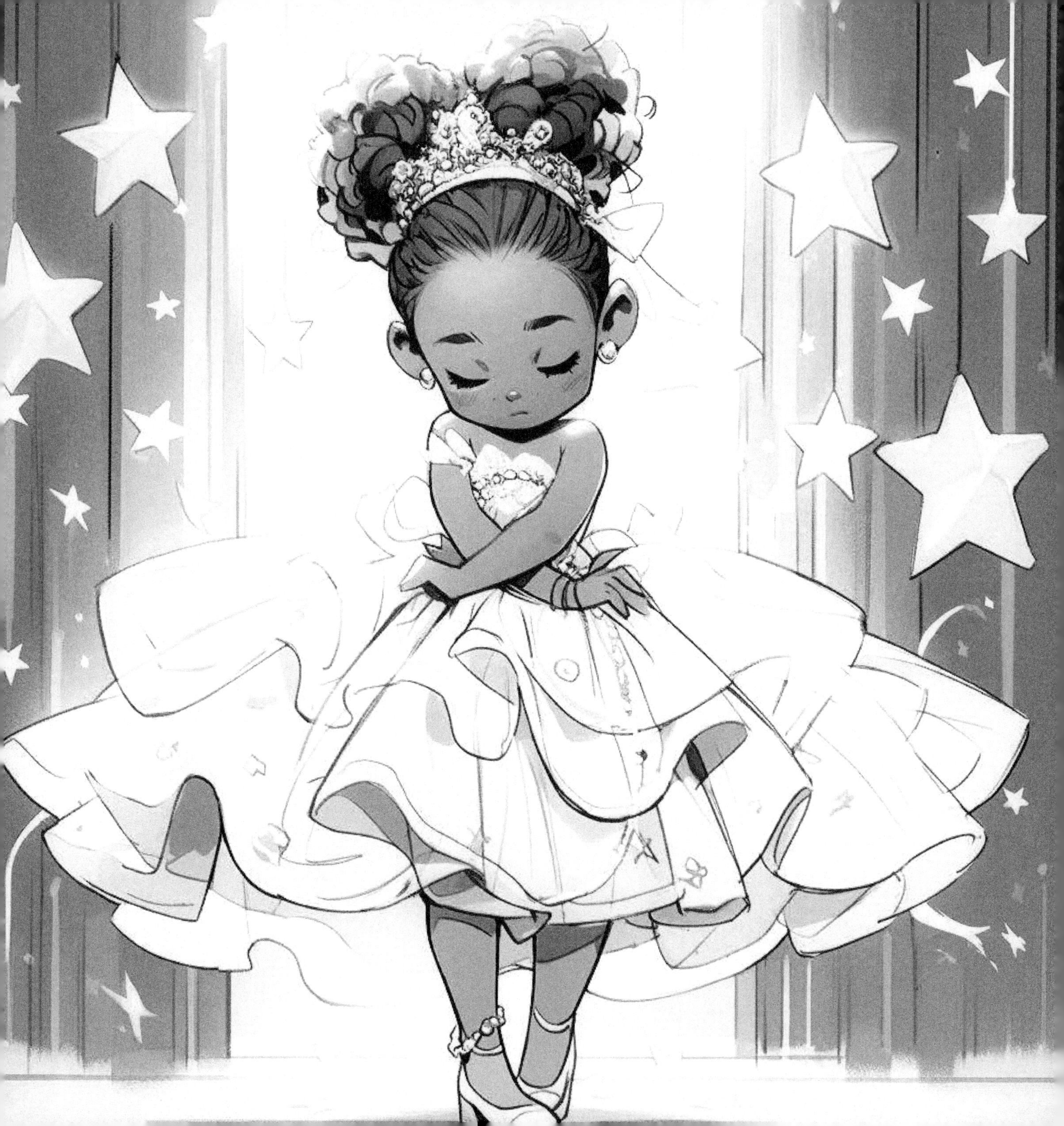

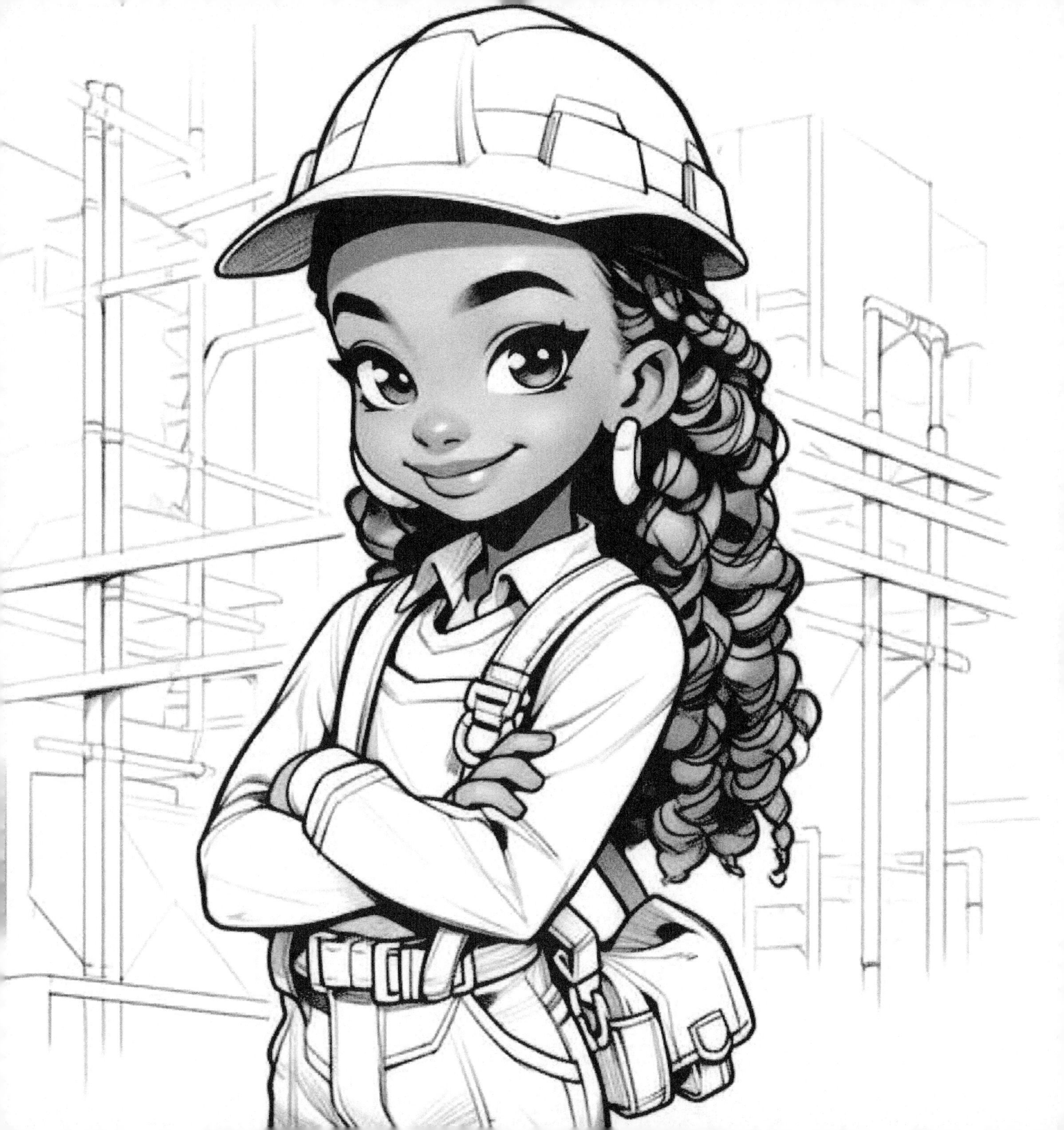

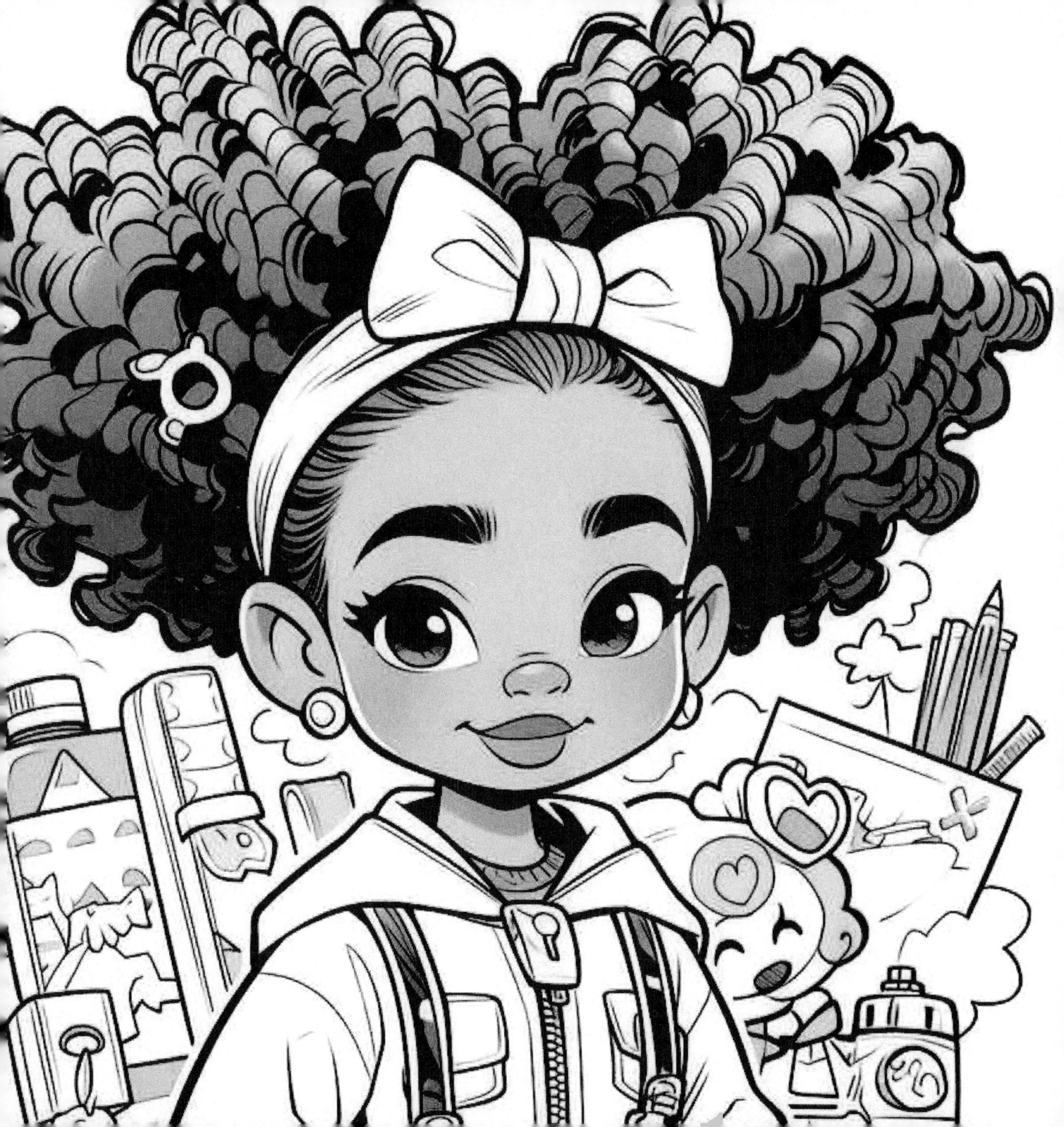

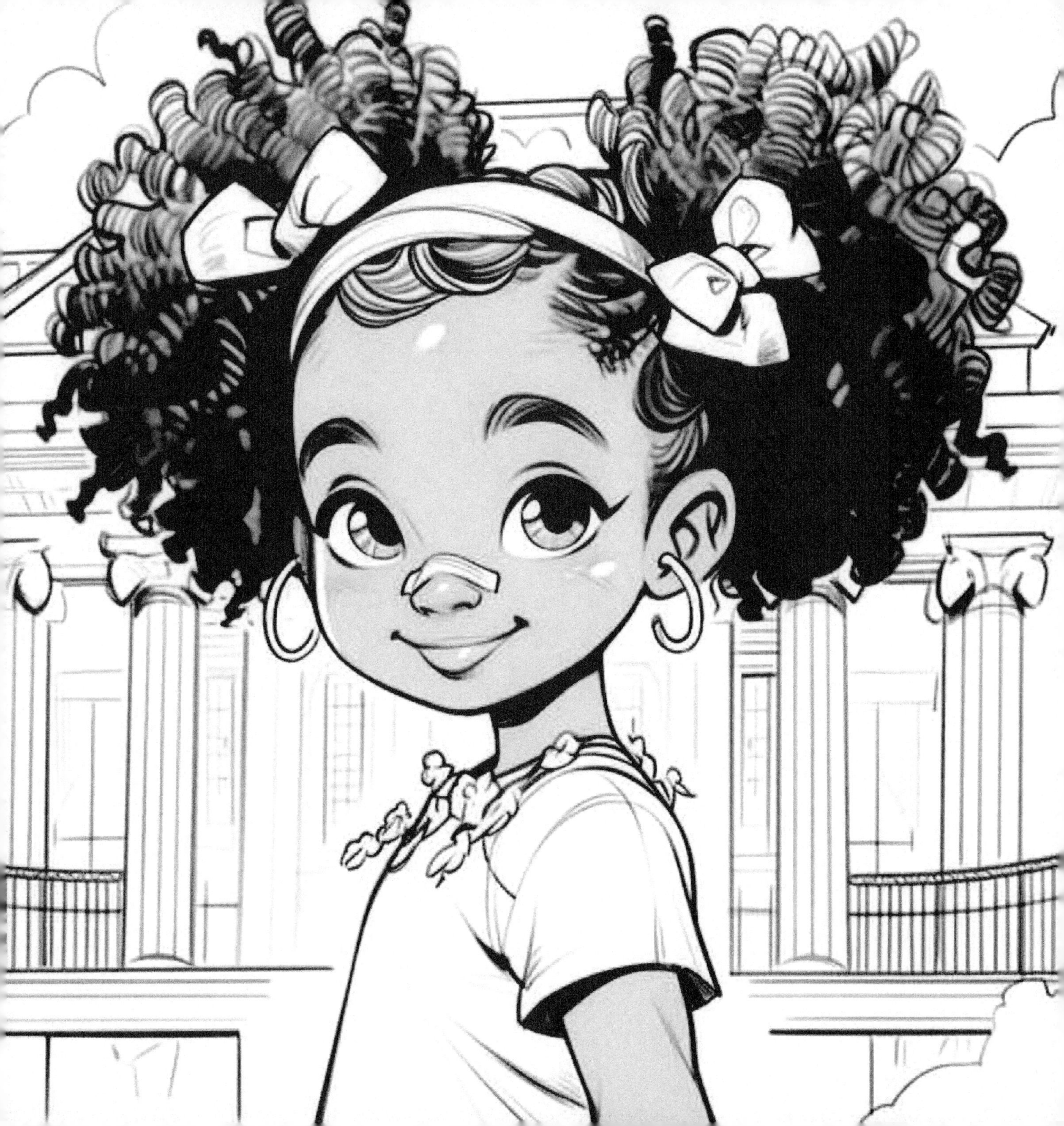

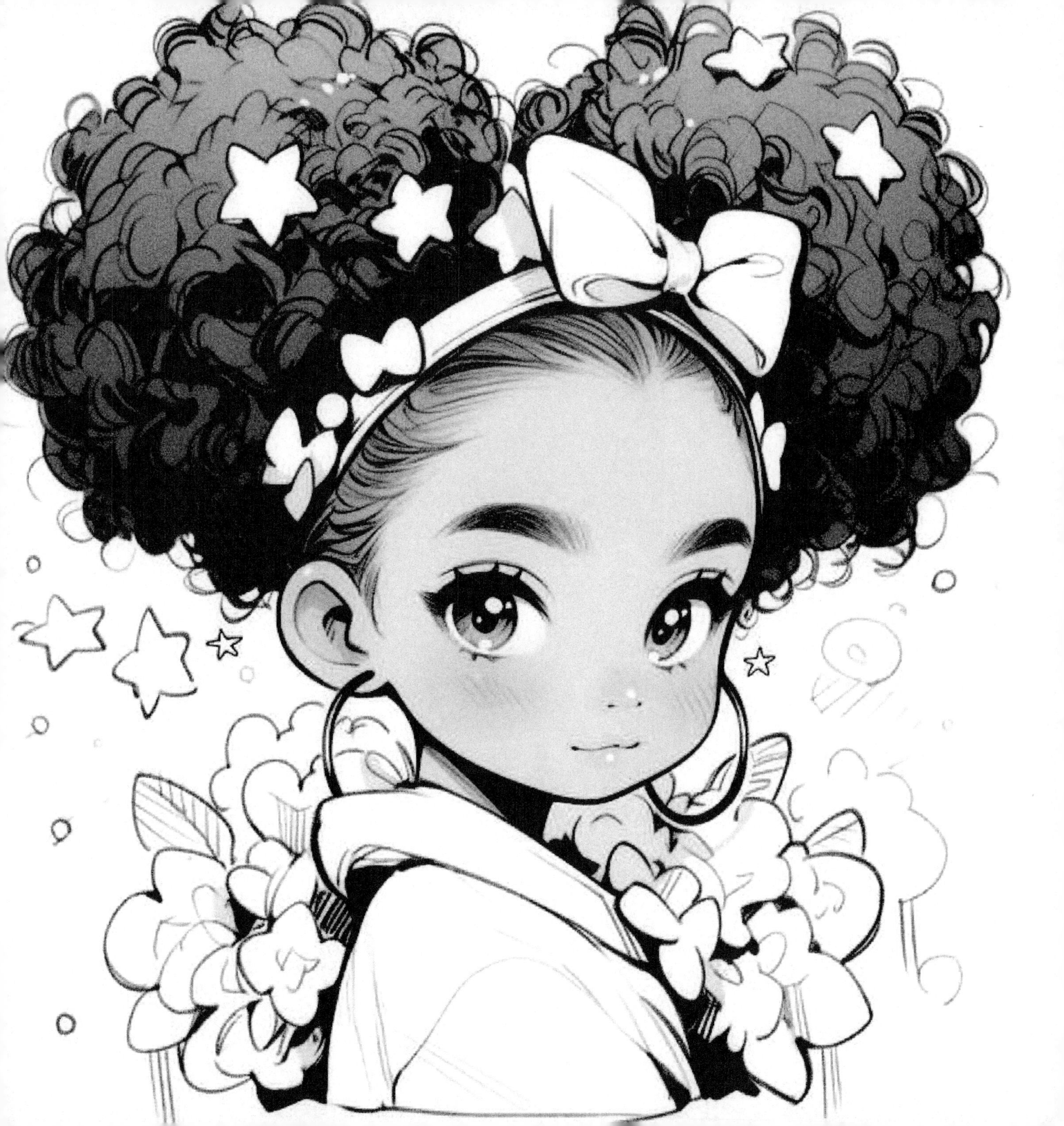

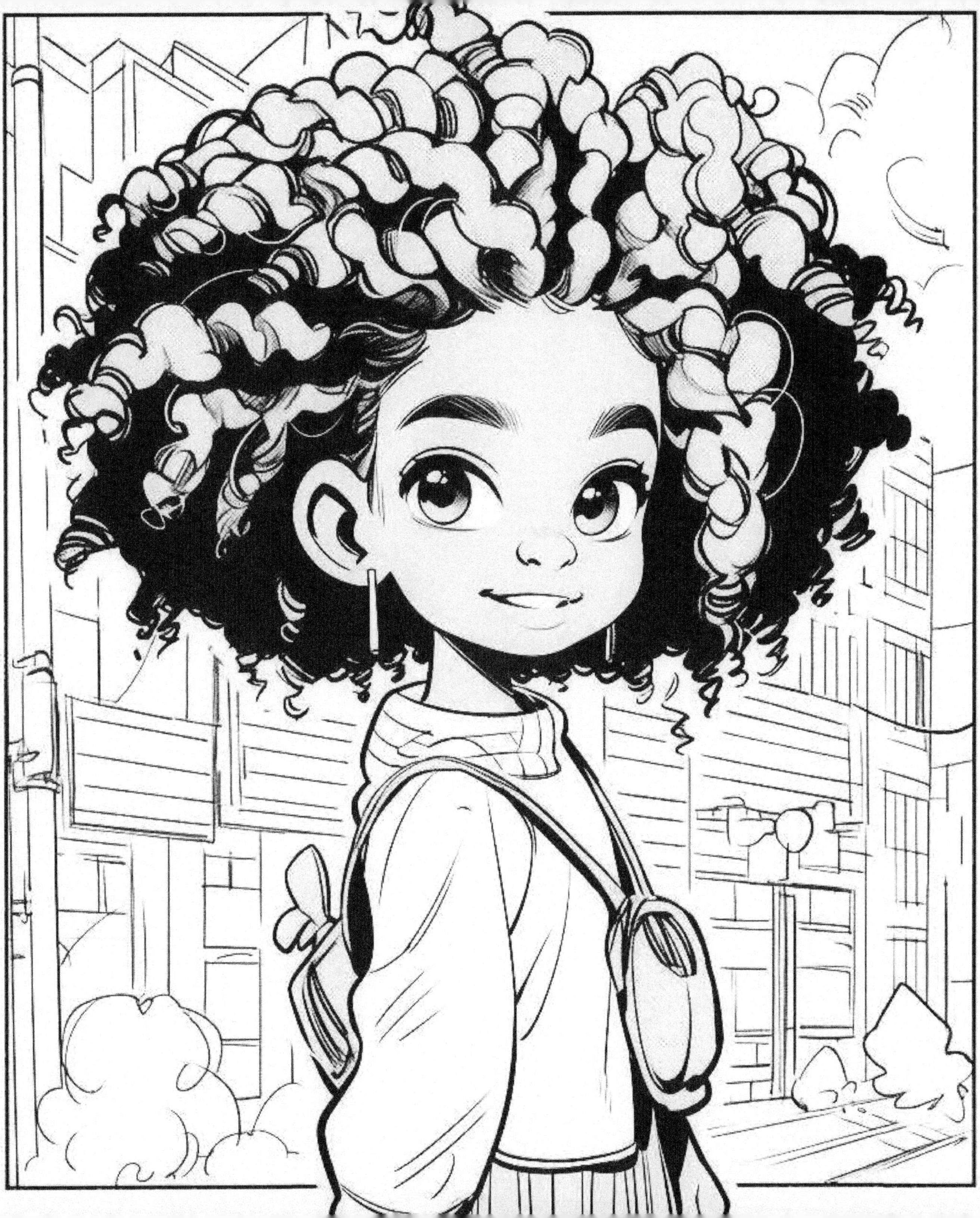

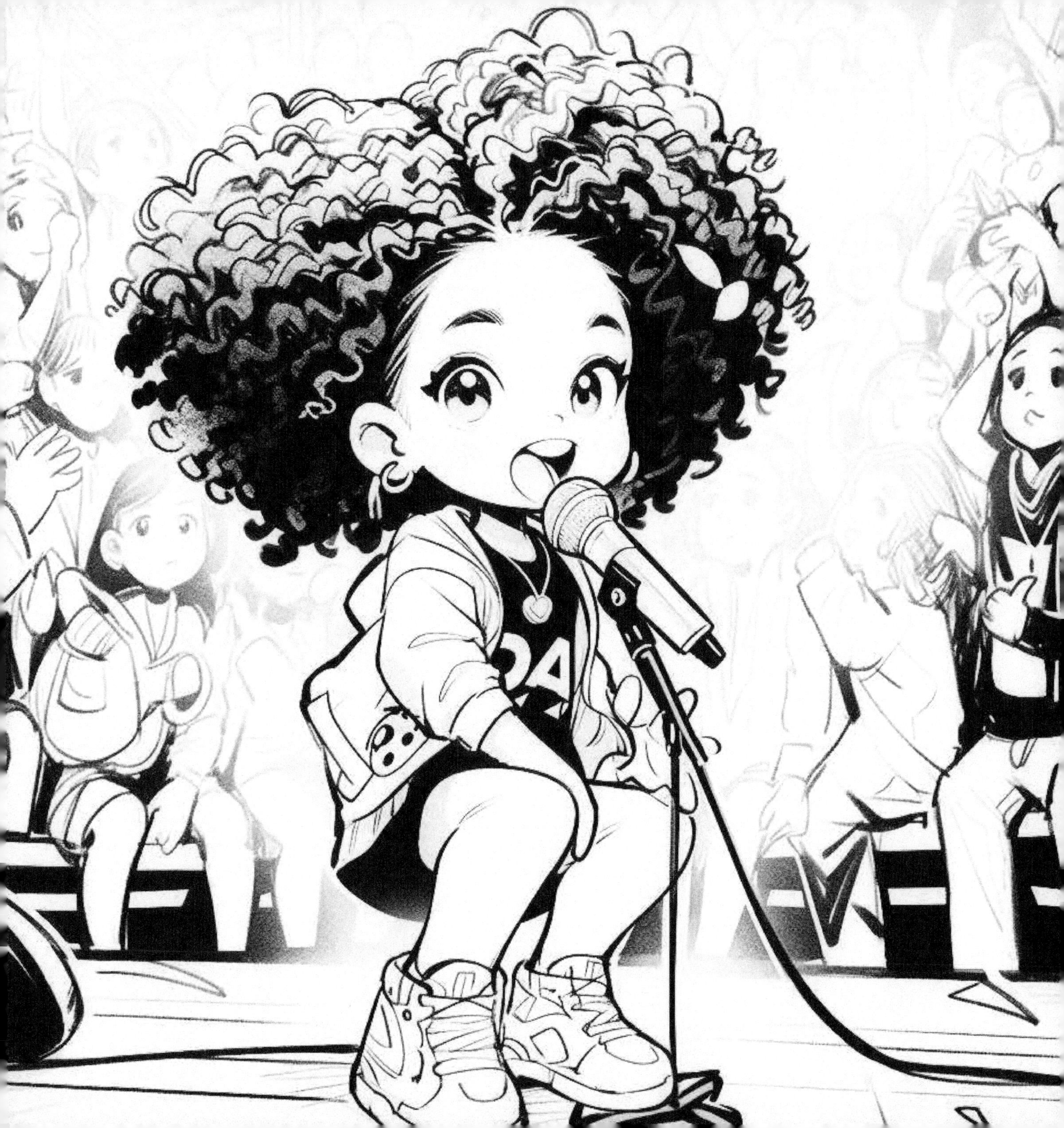

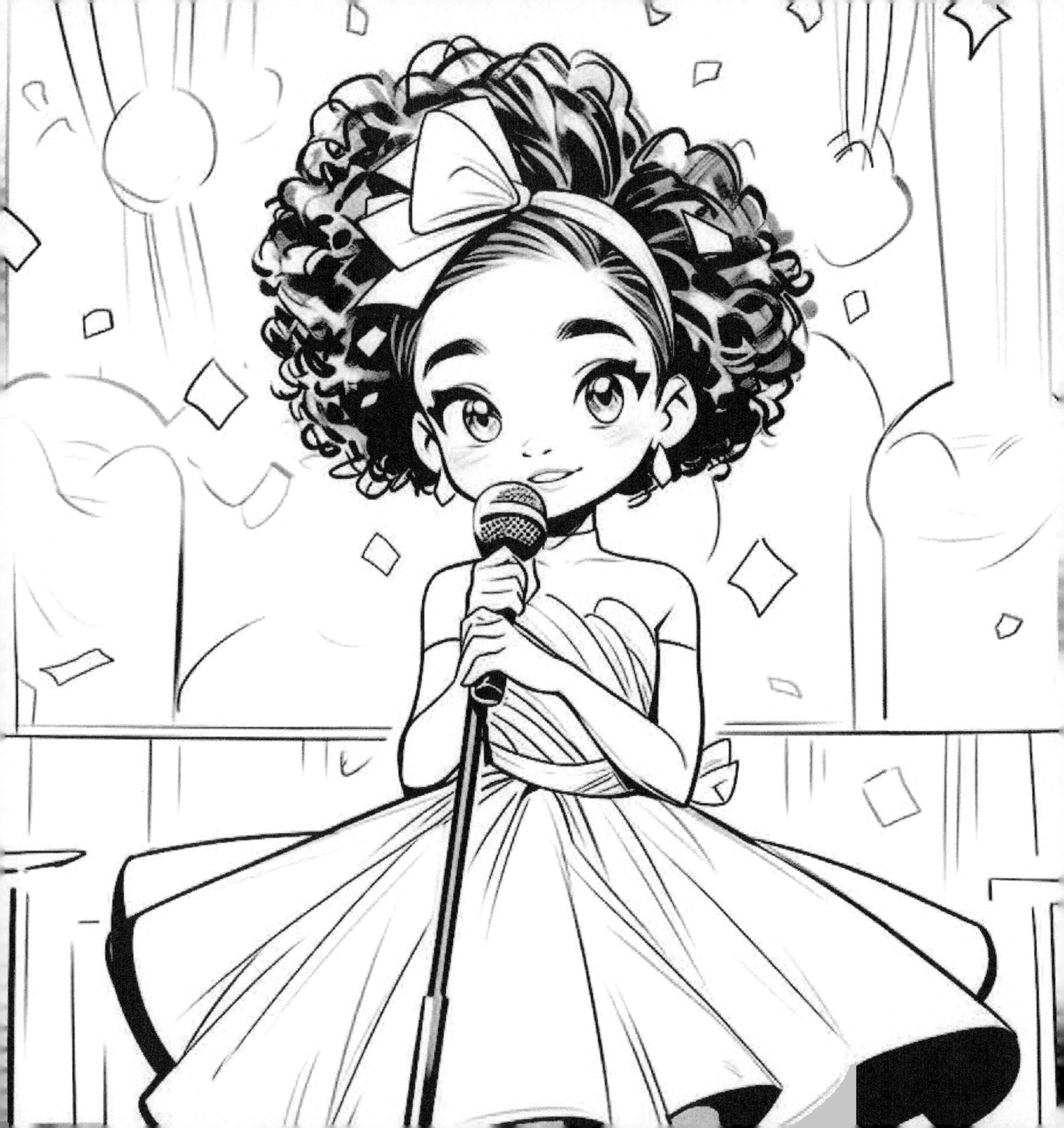

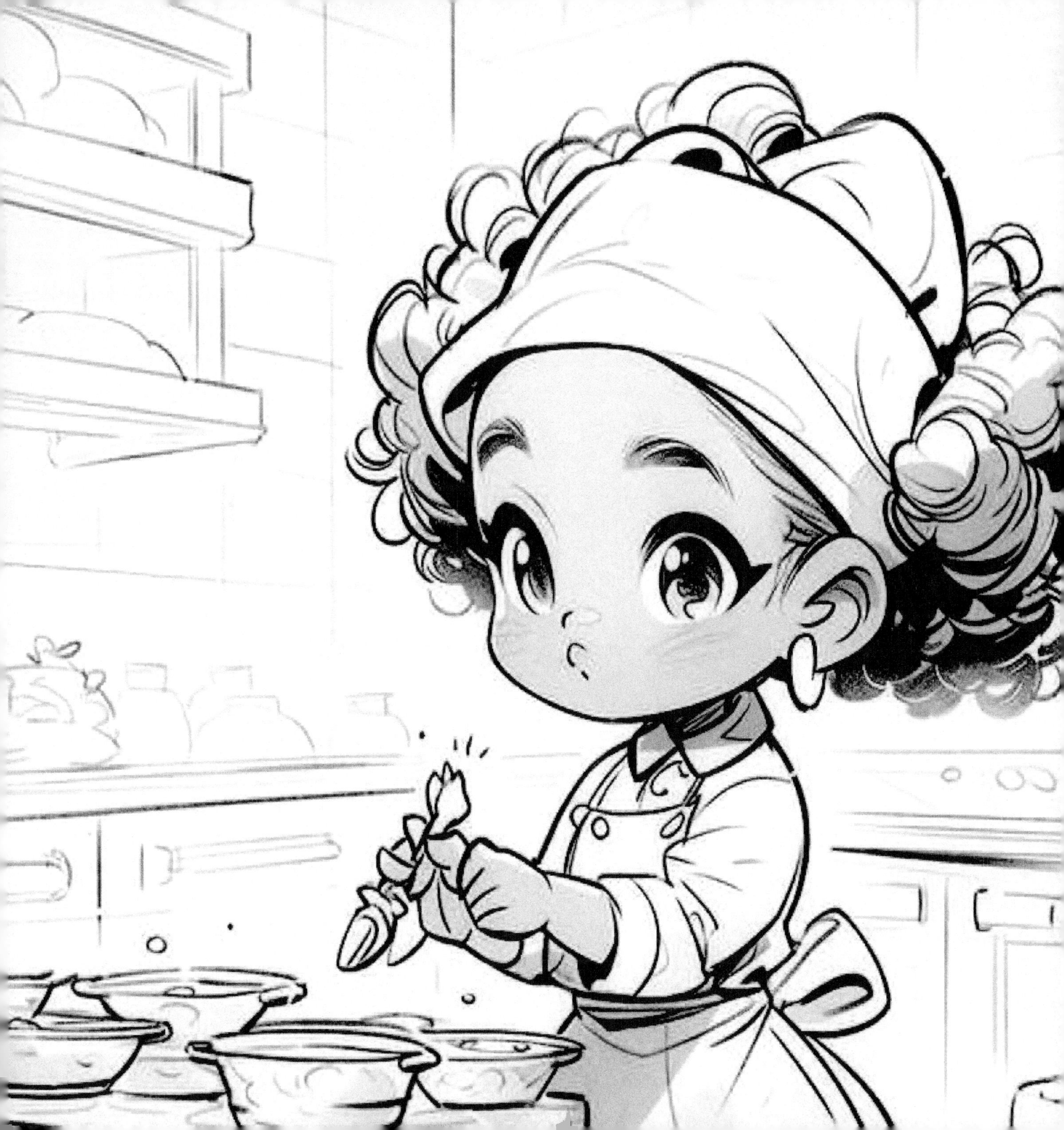

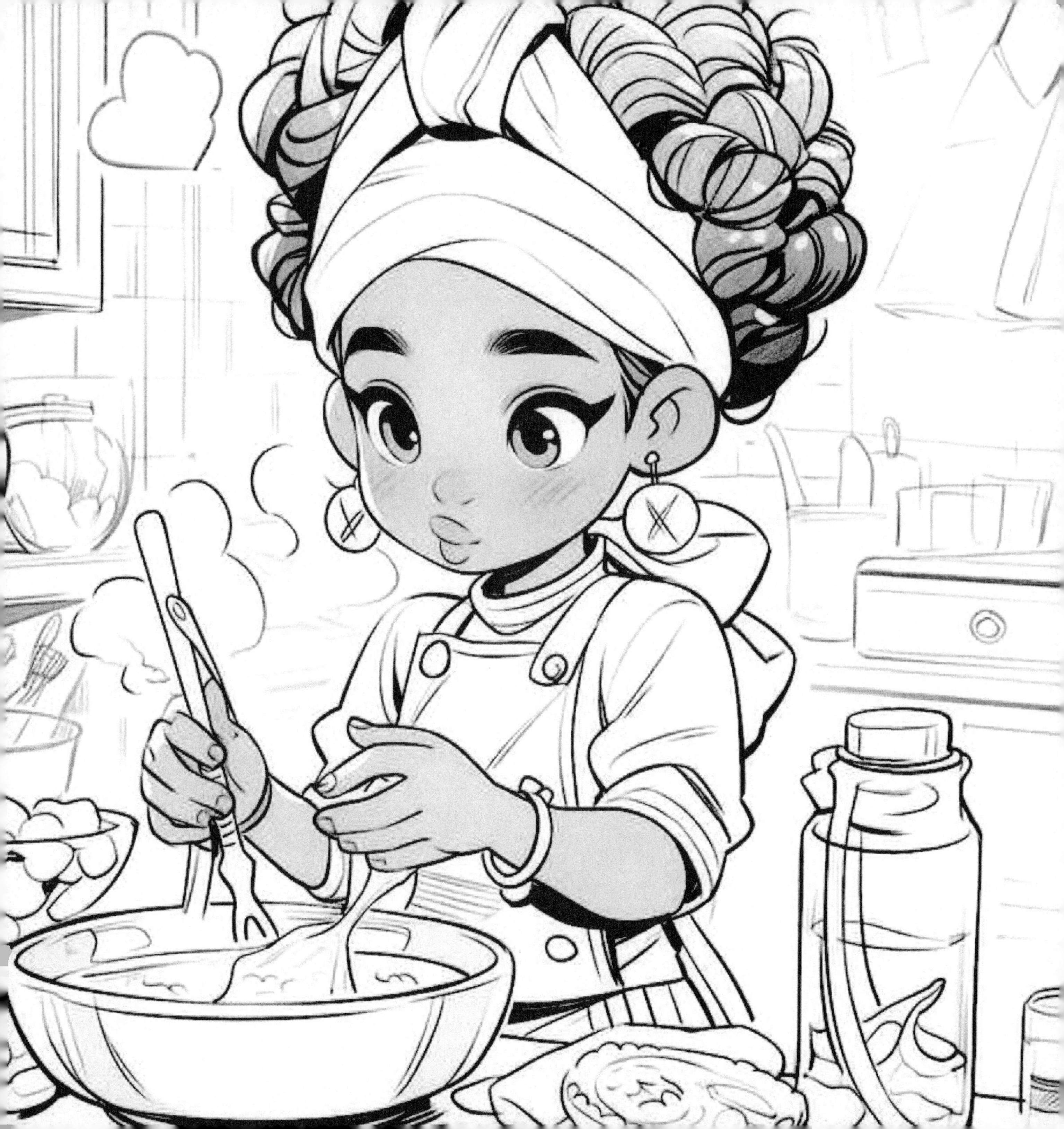

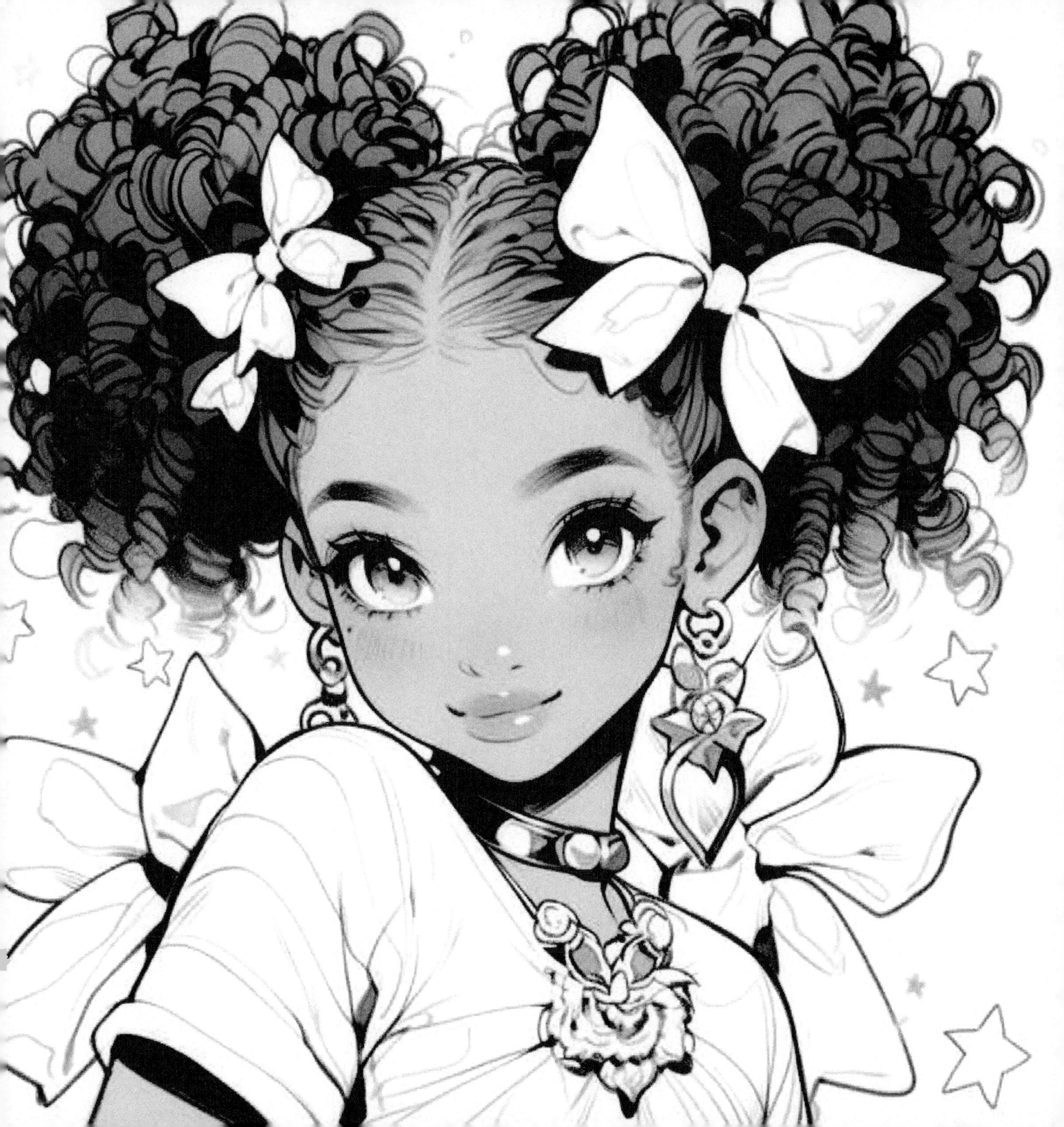

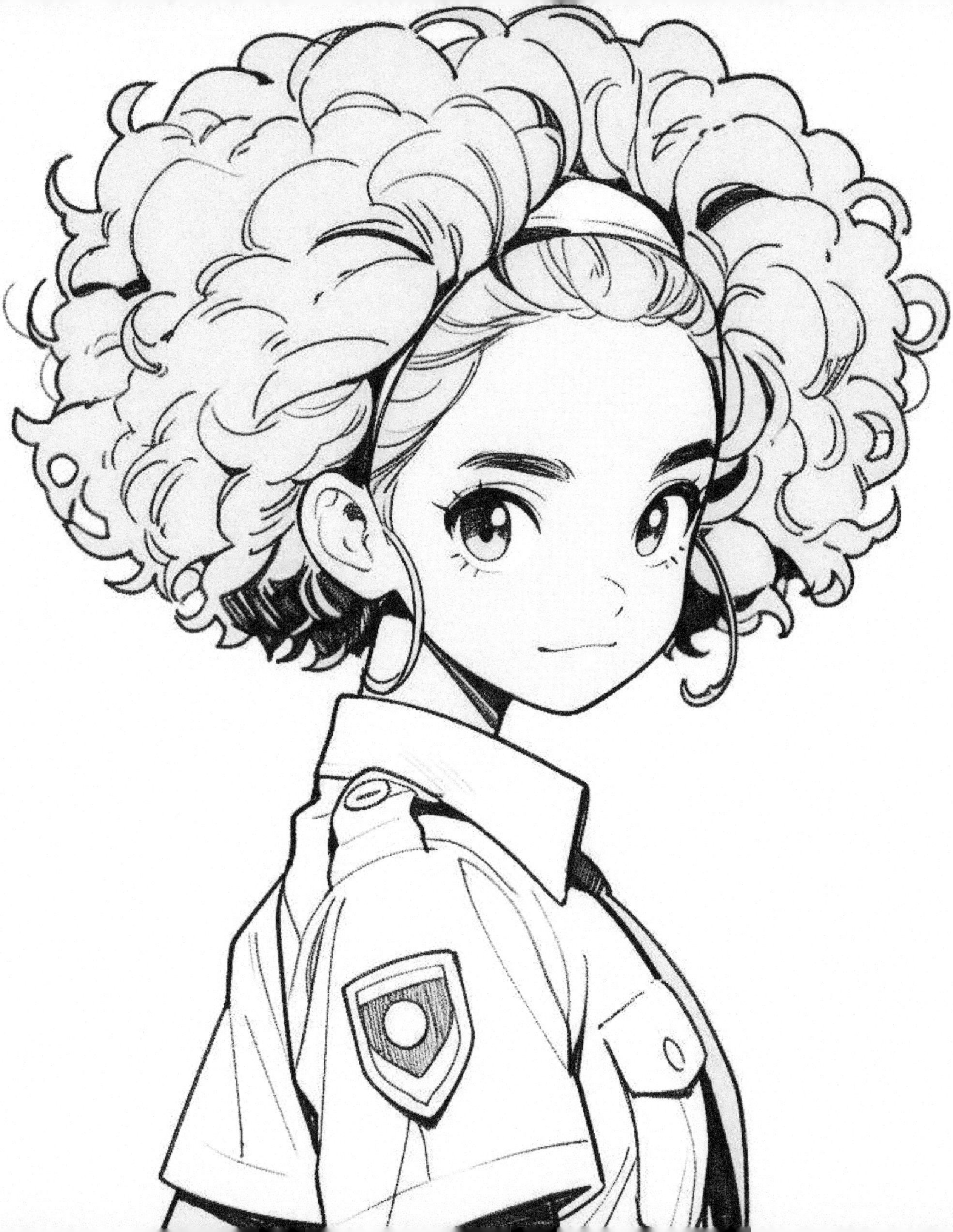

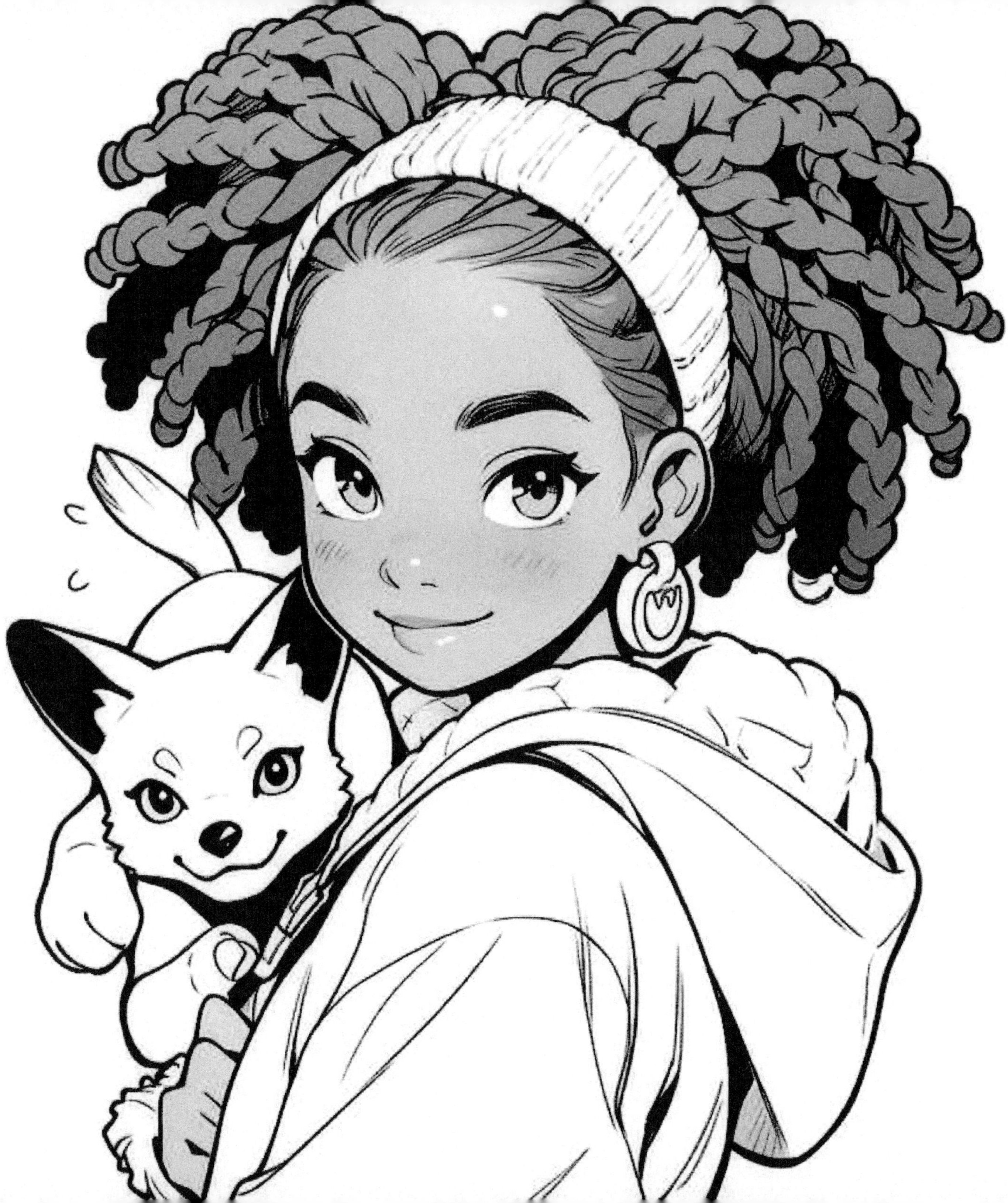

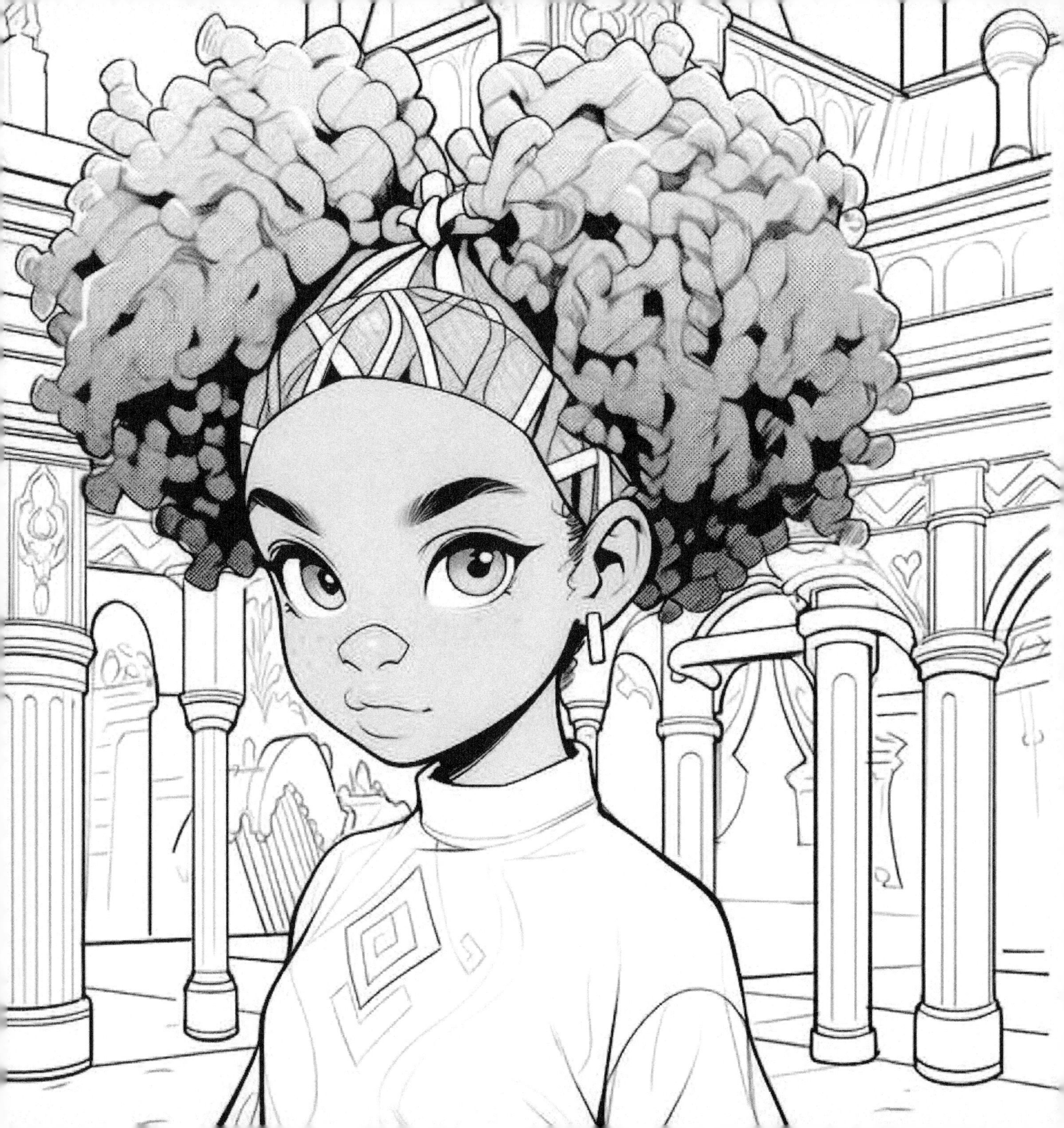

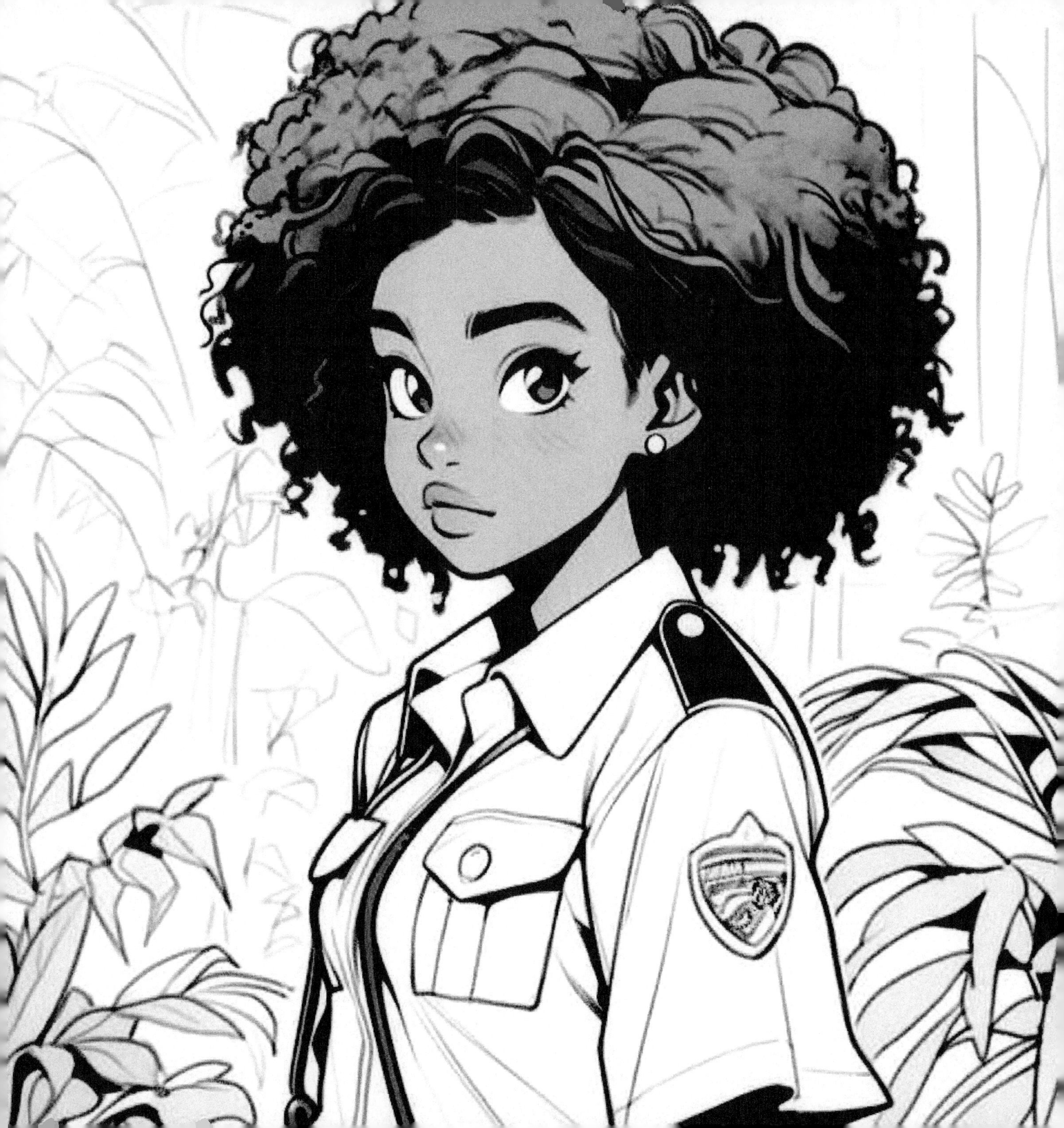

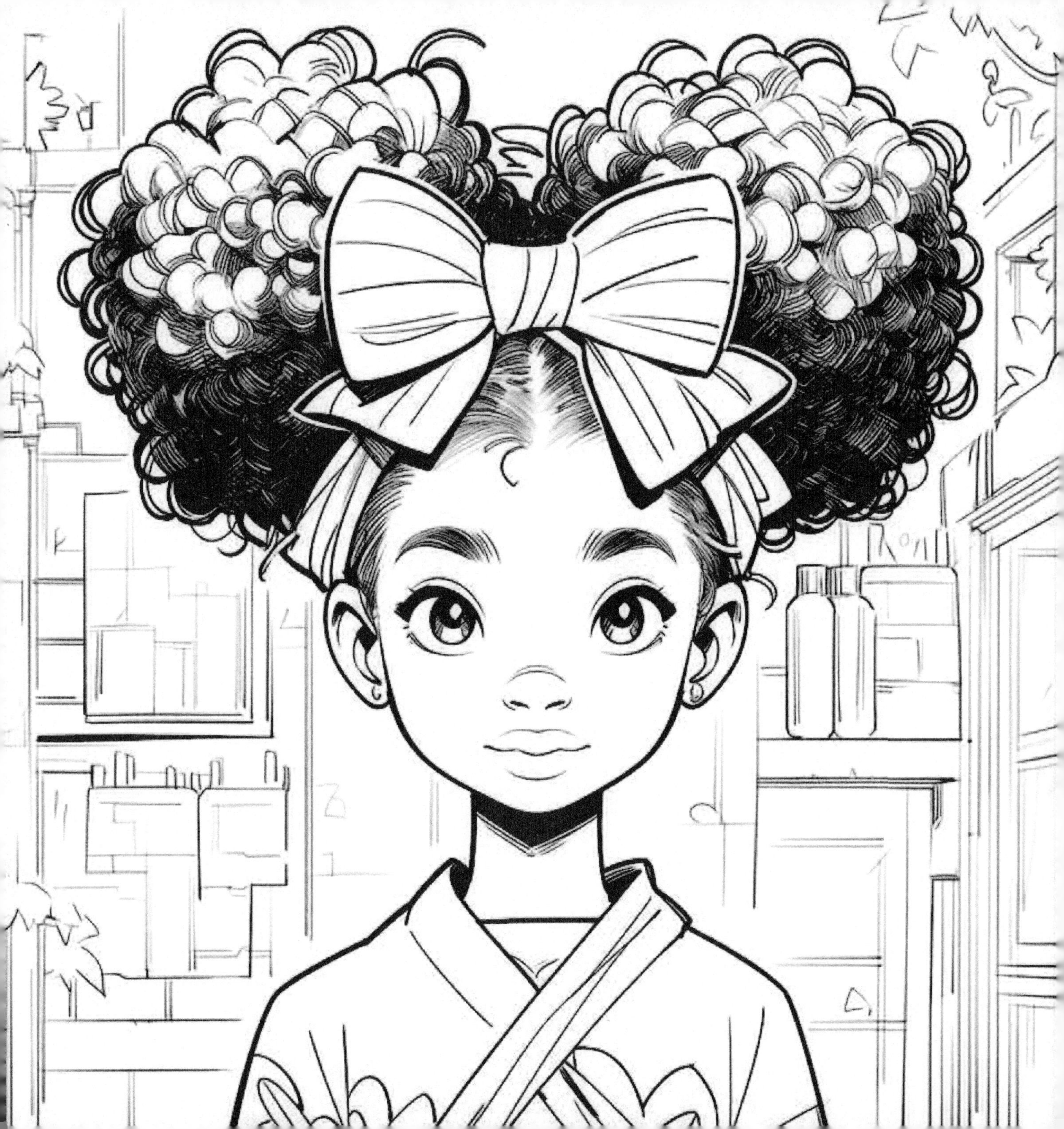

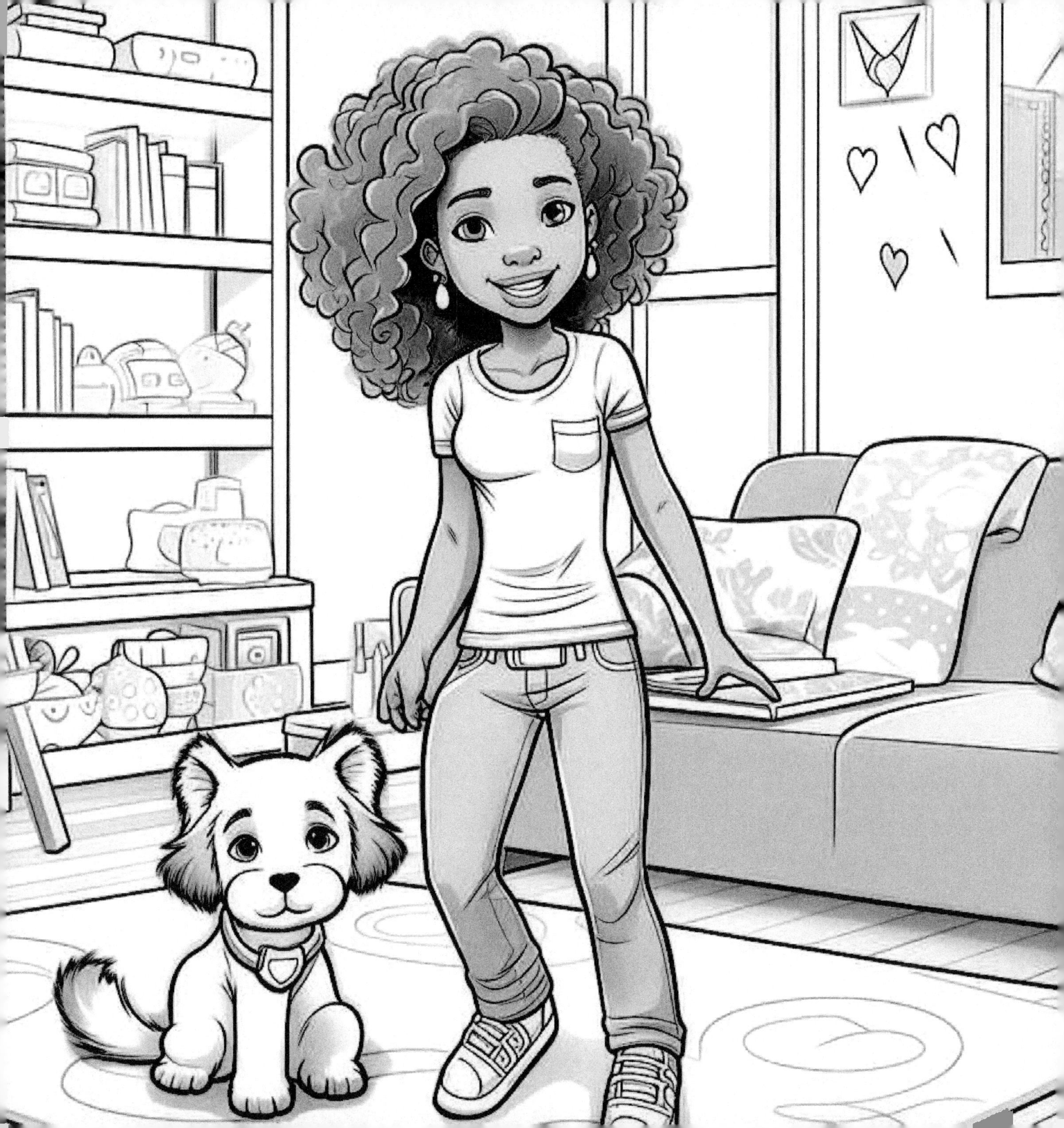

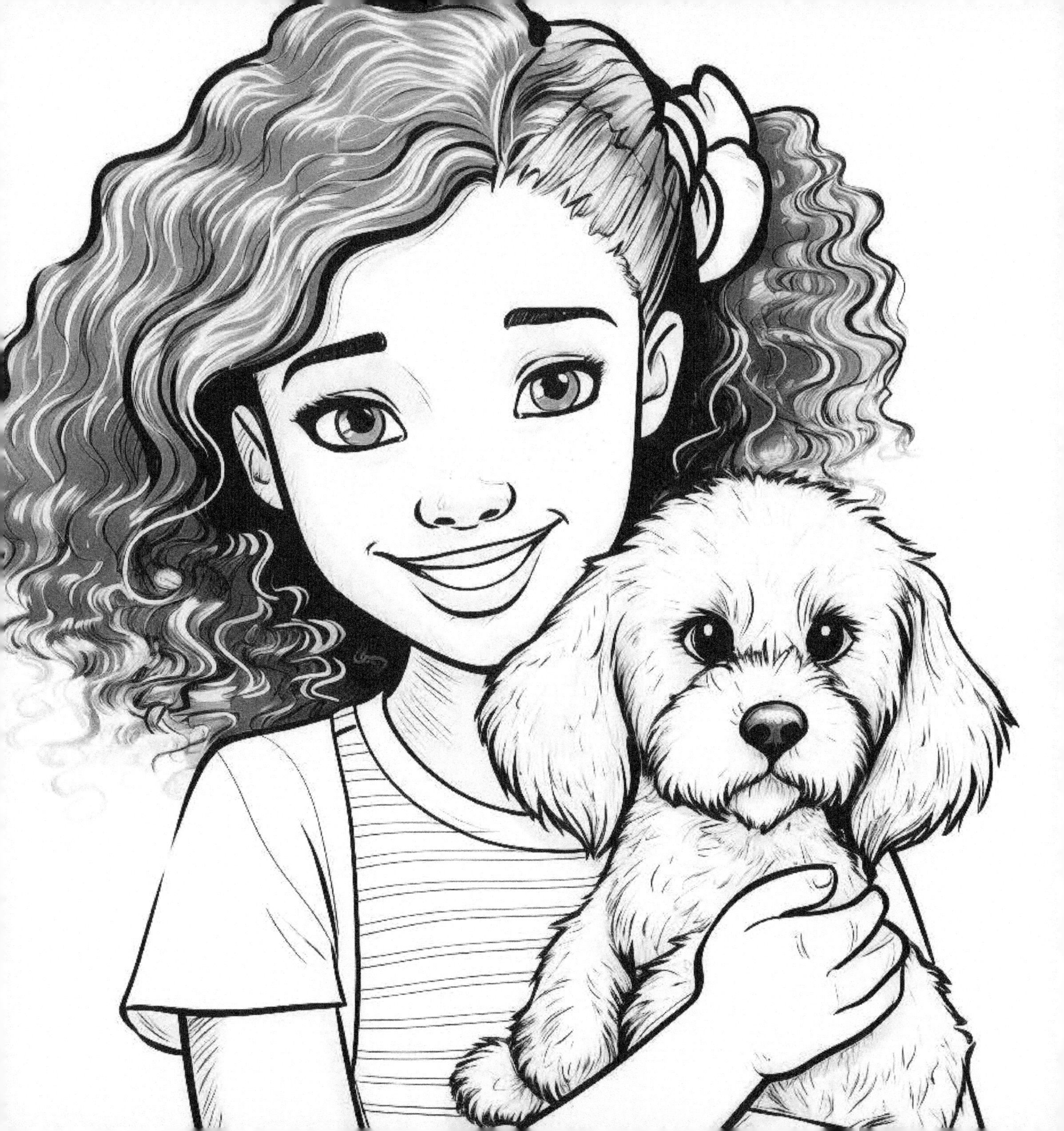

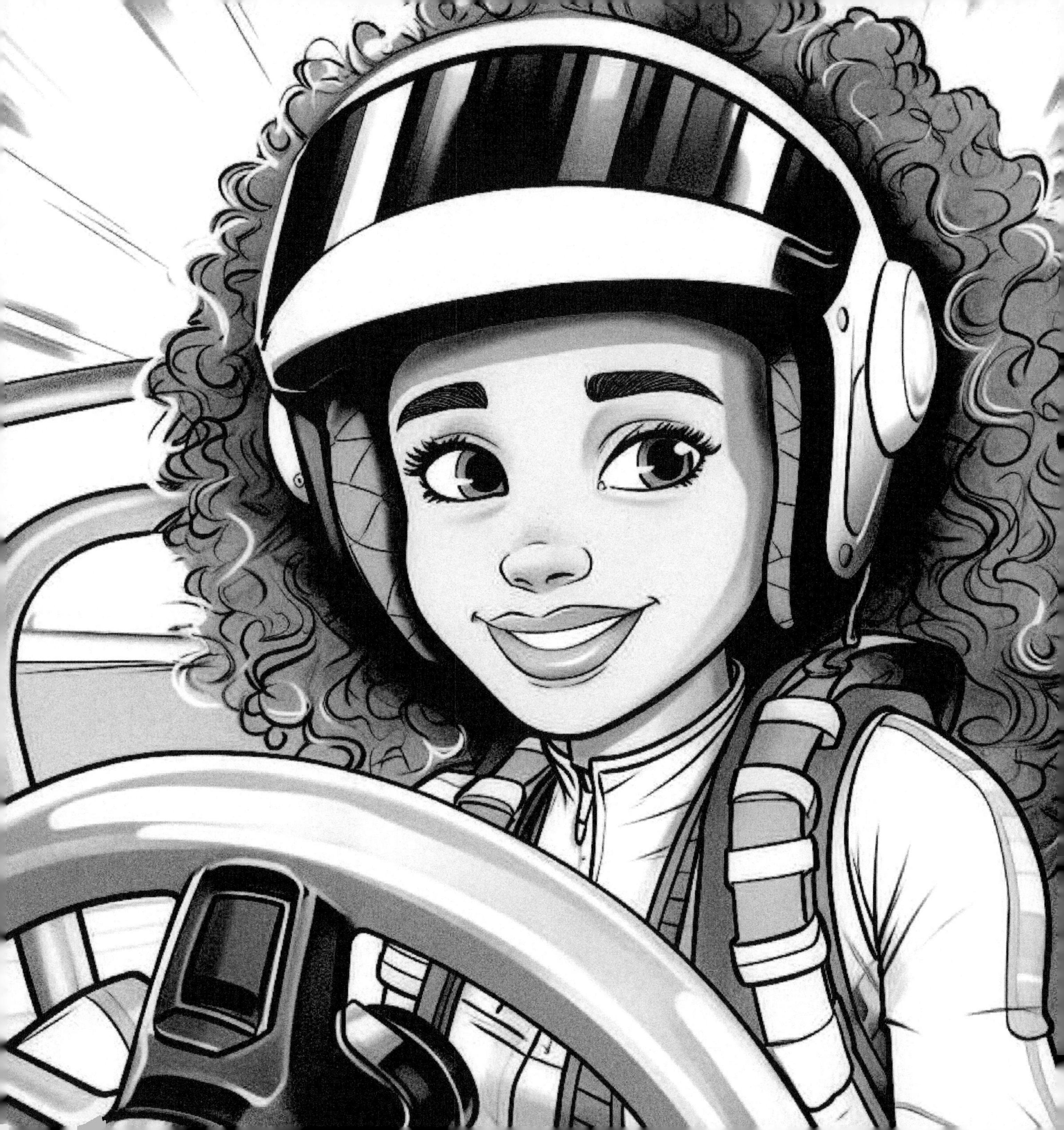

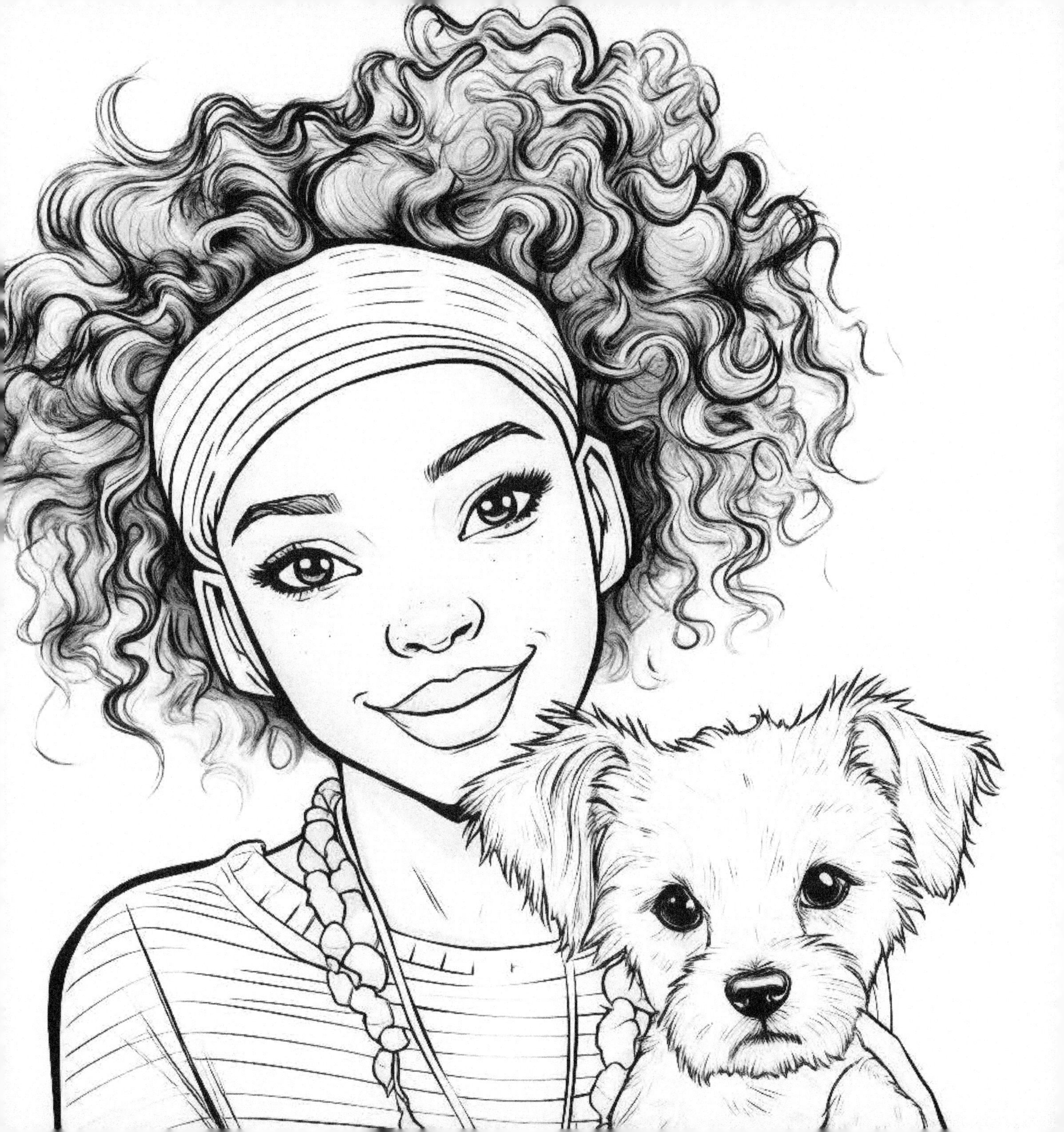

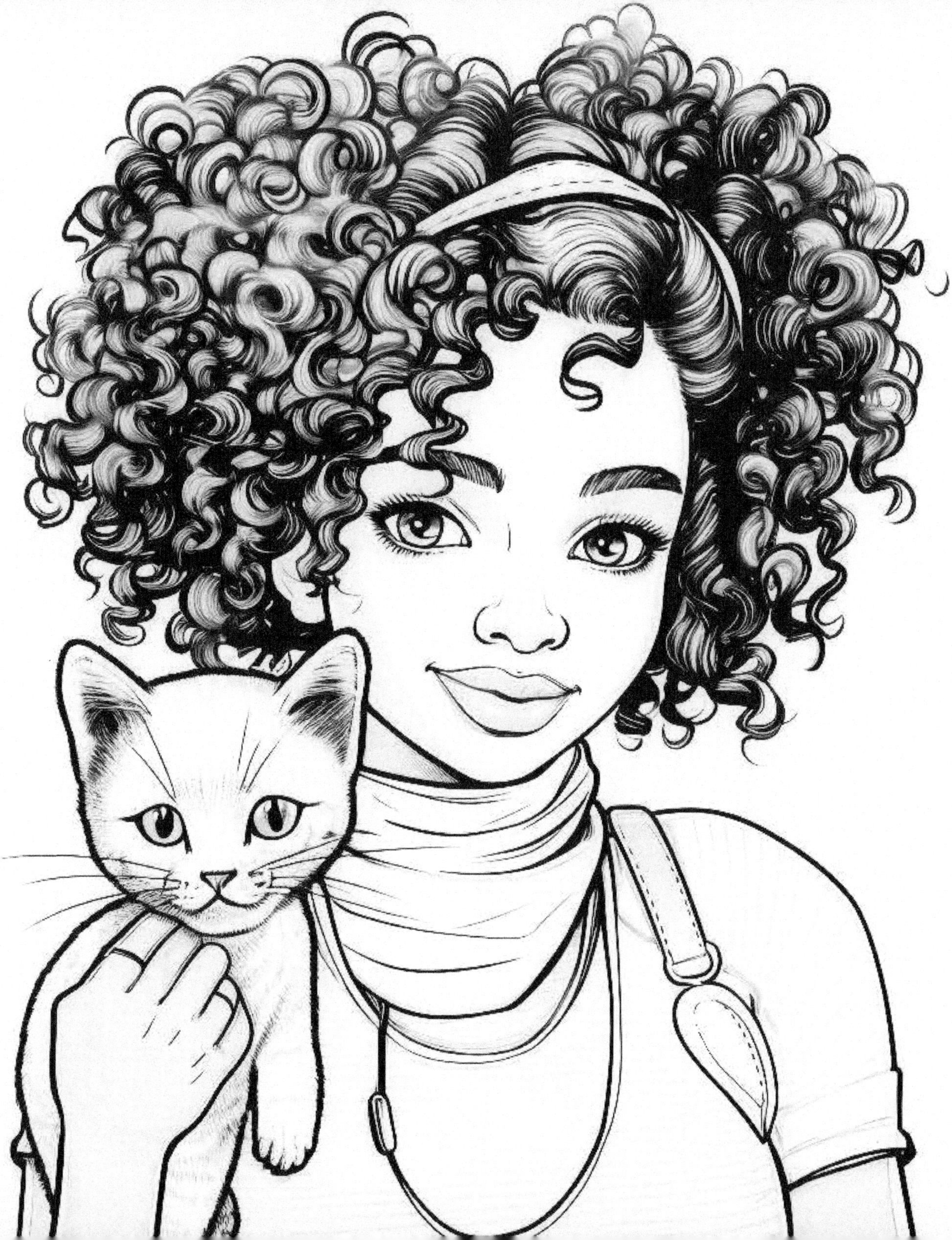

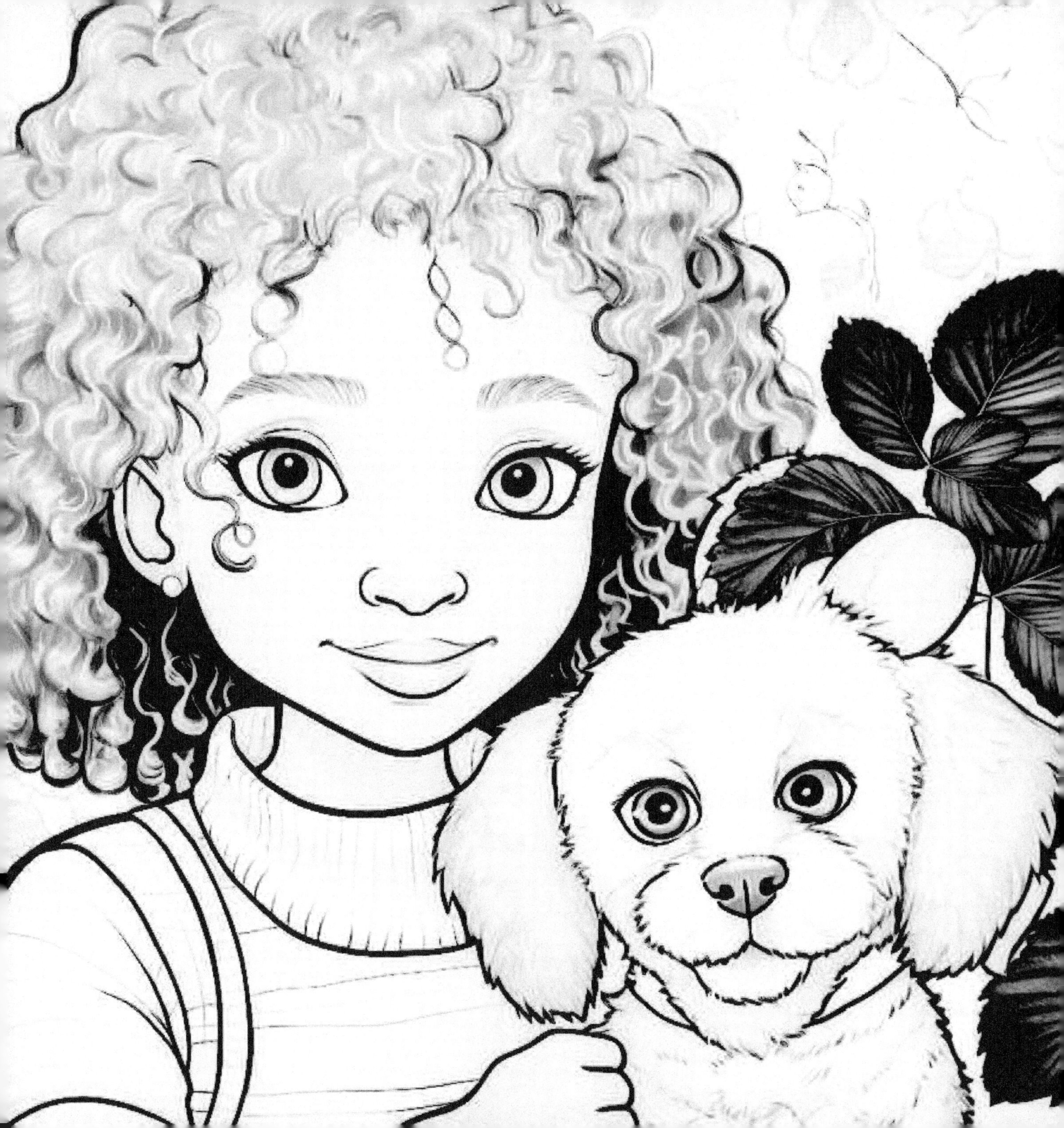

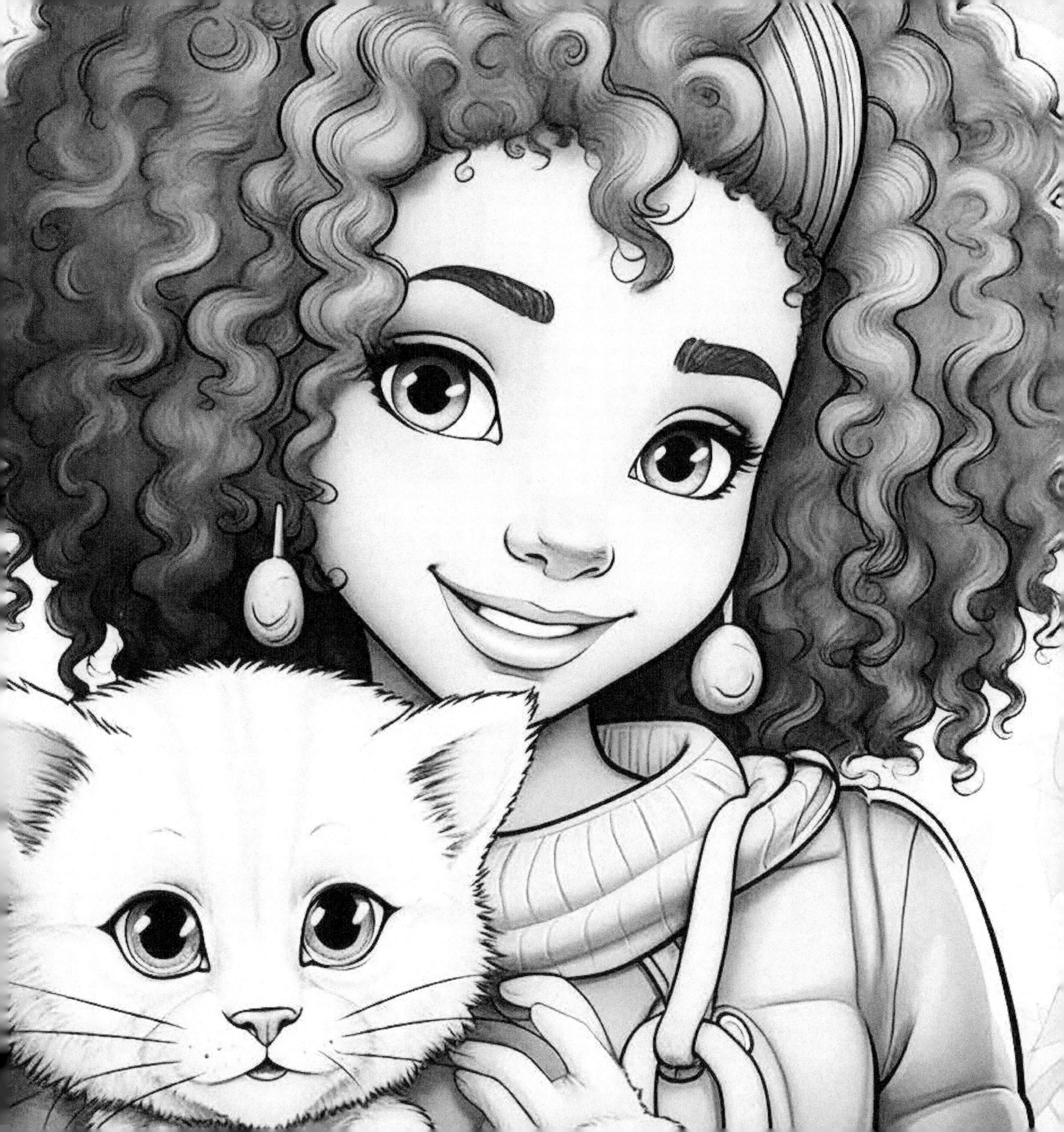

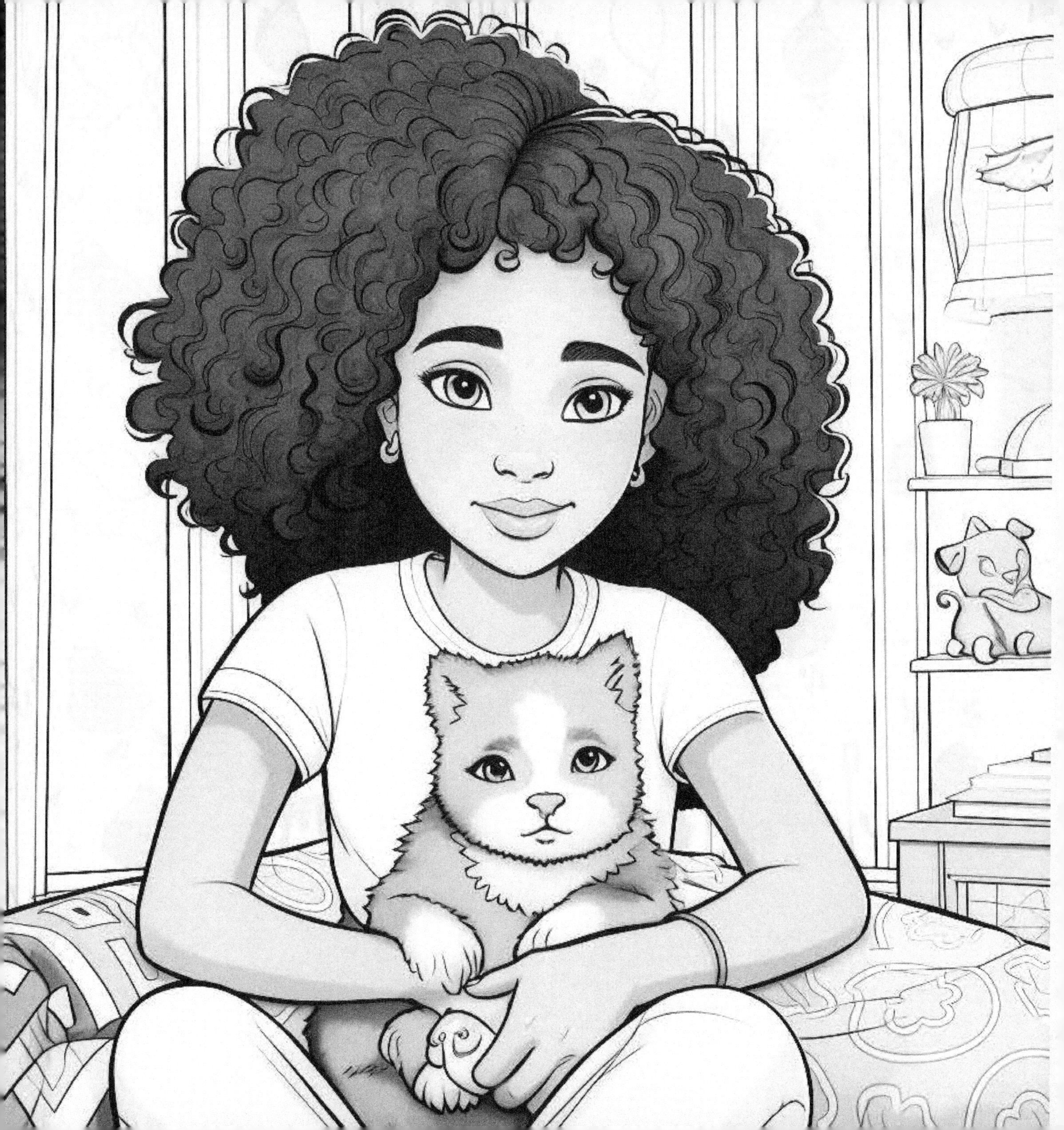

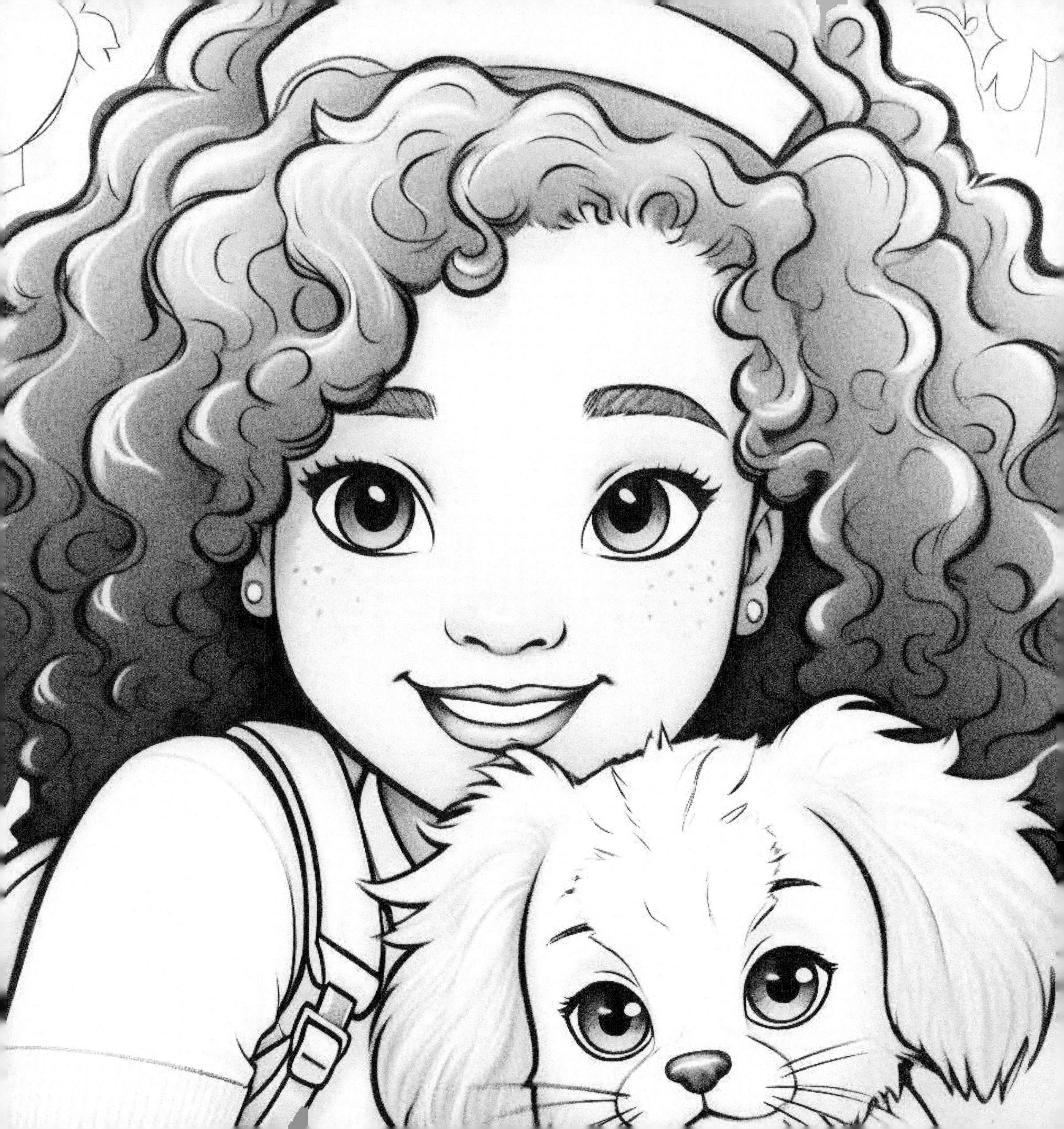

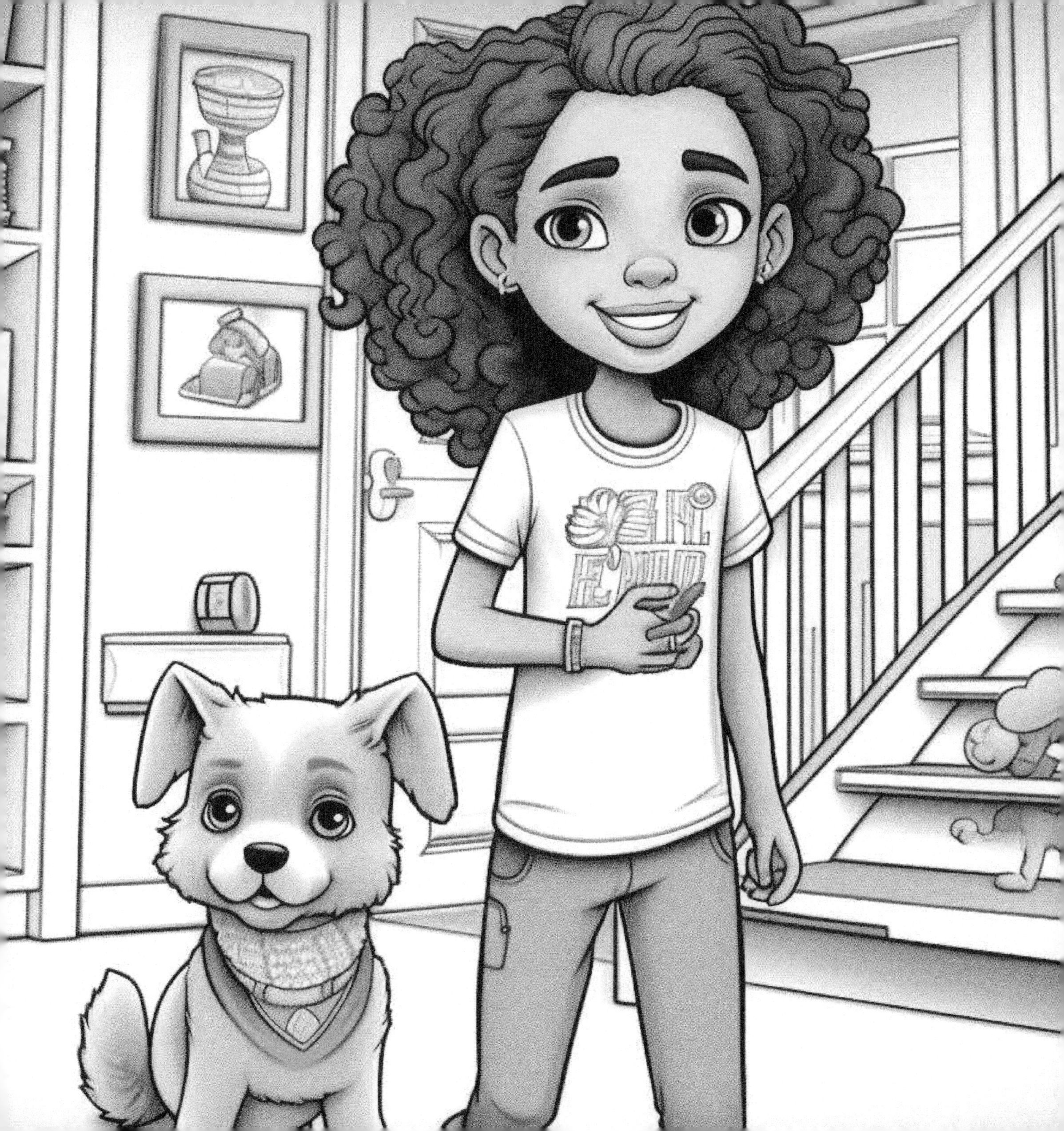

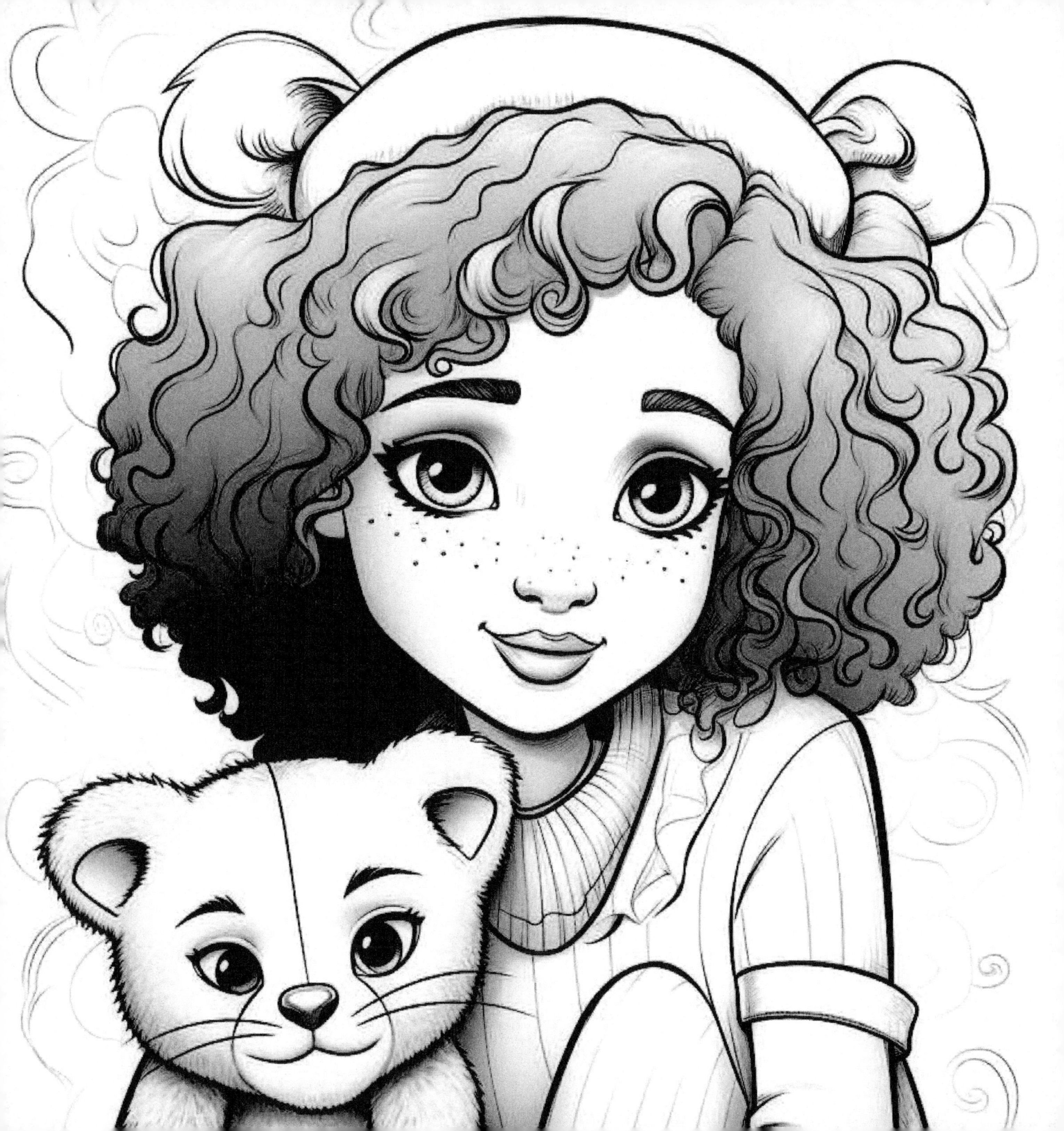

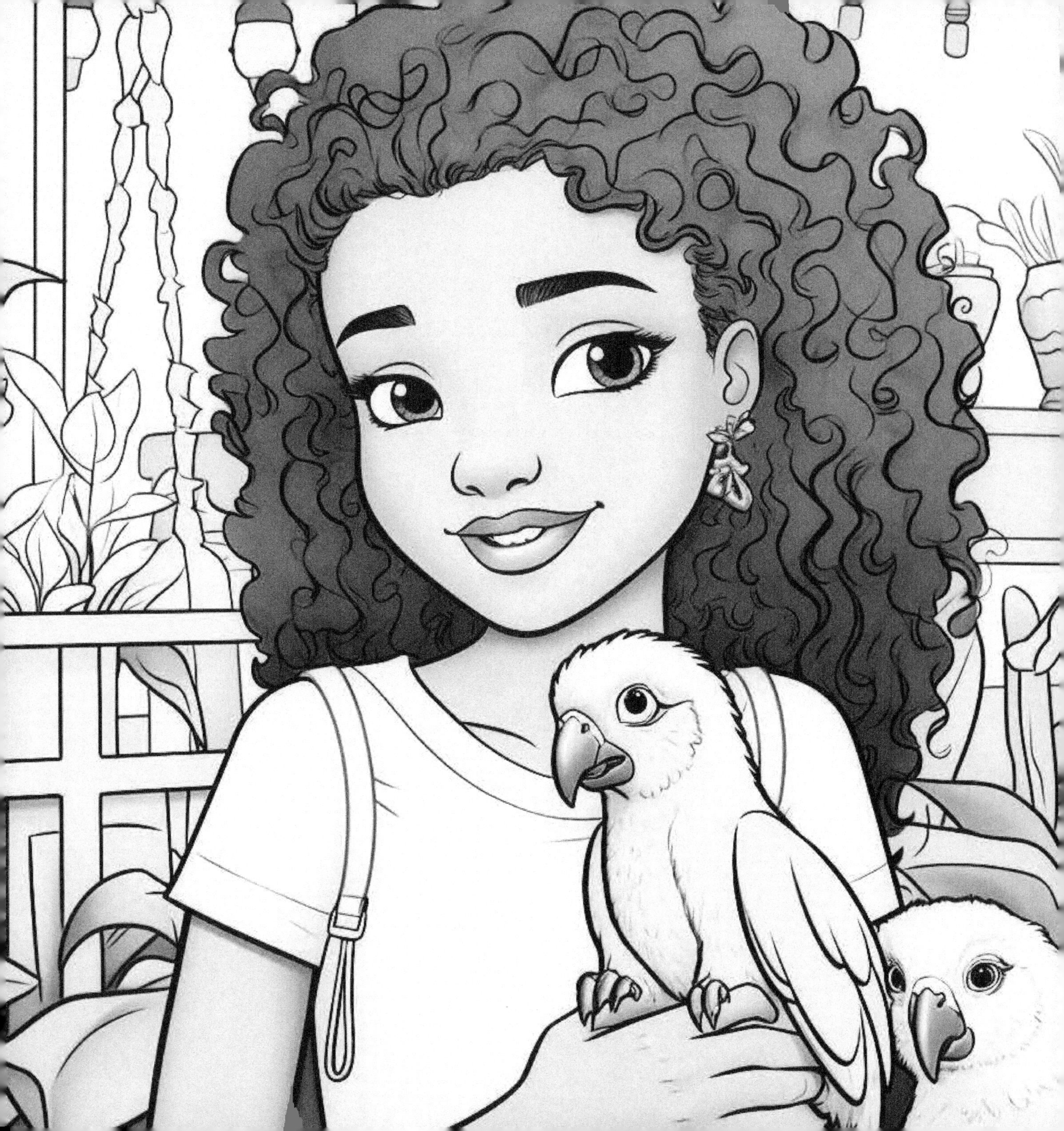

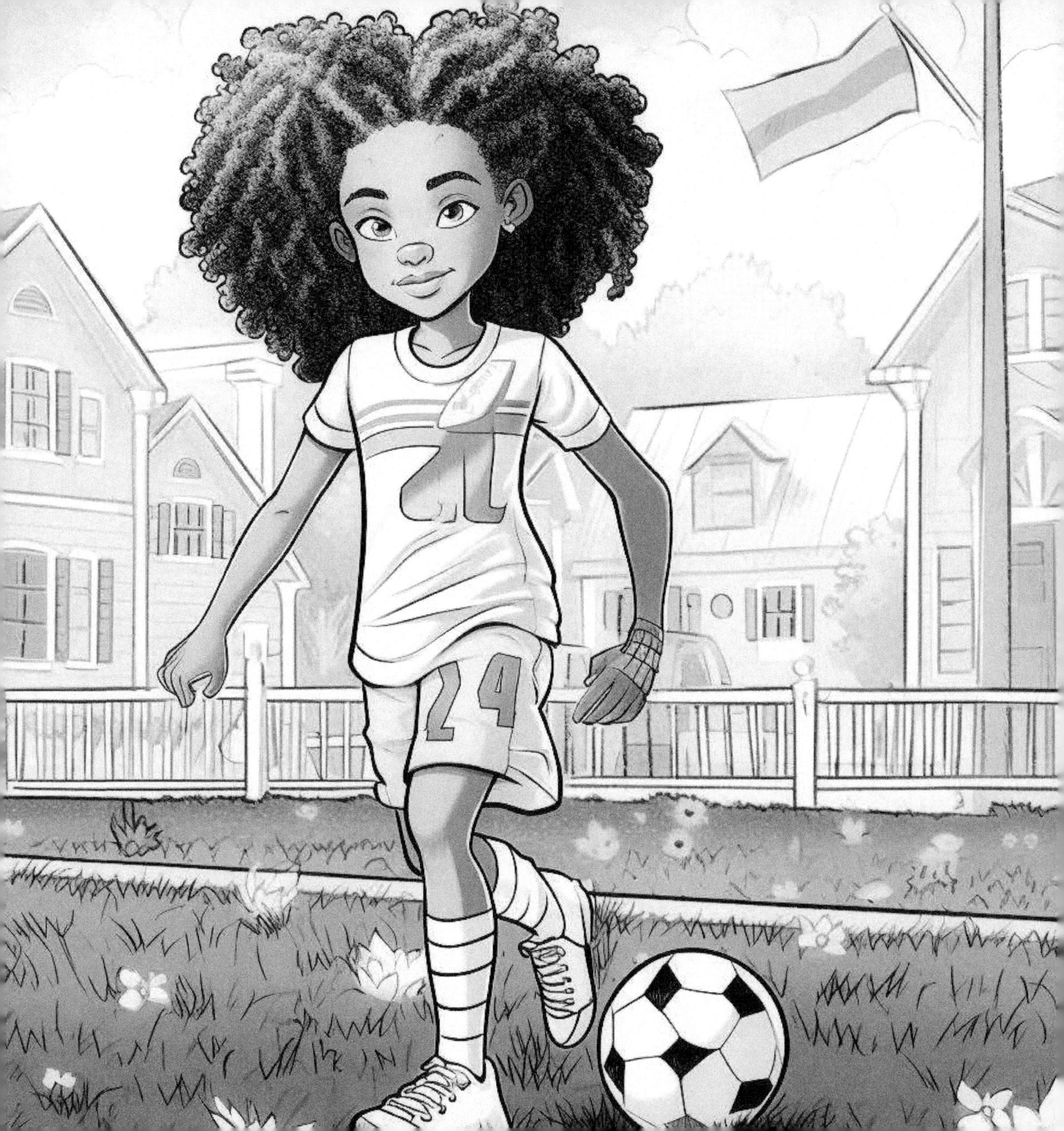
24

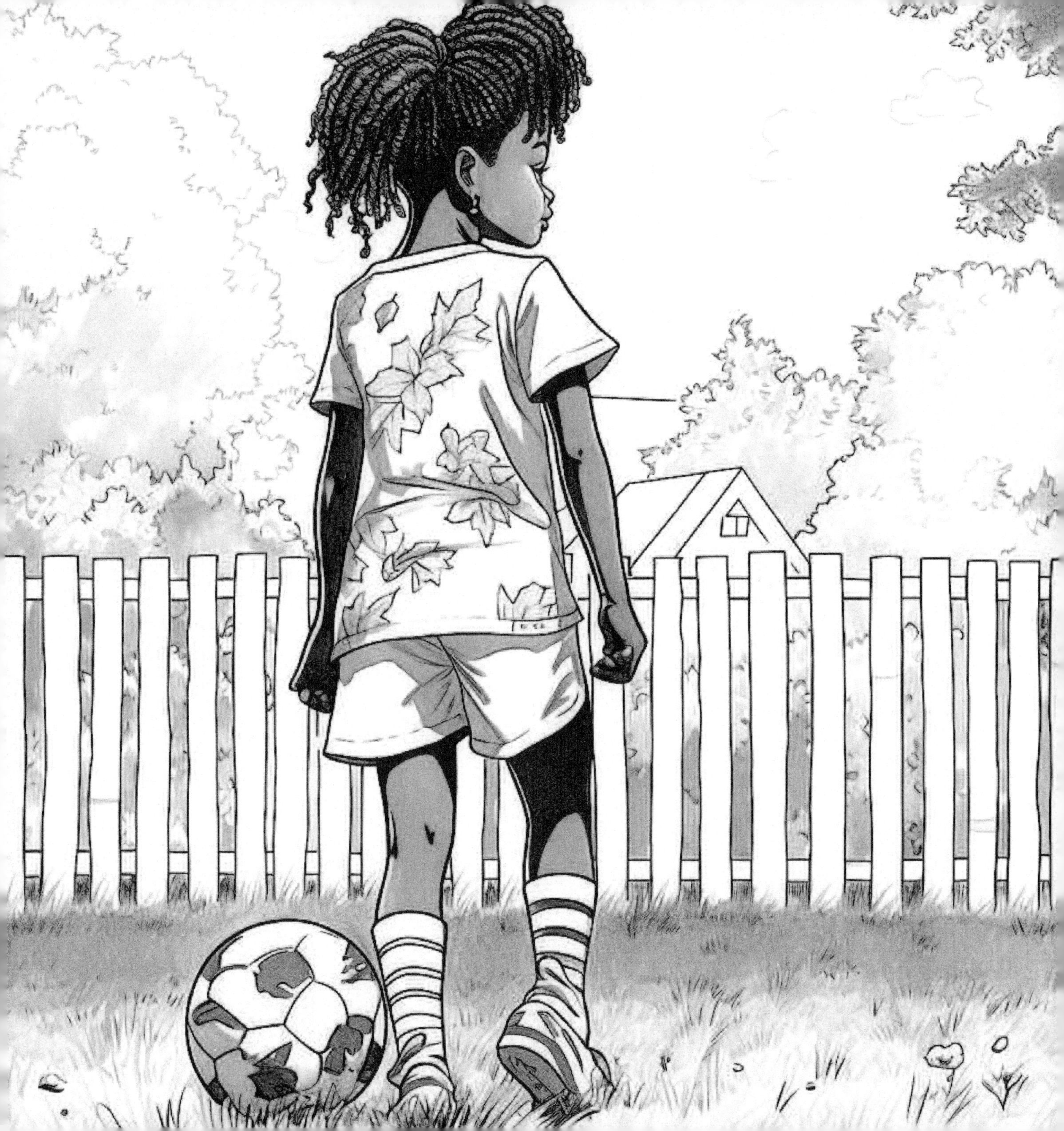

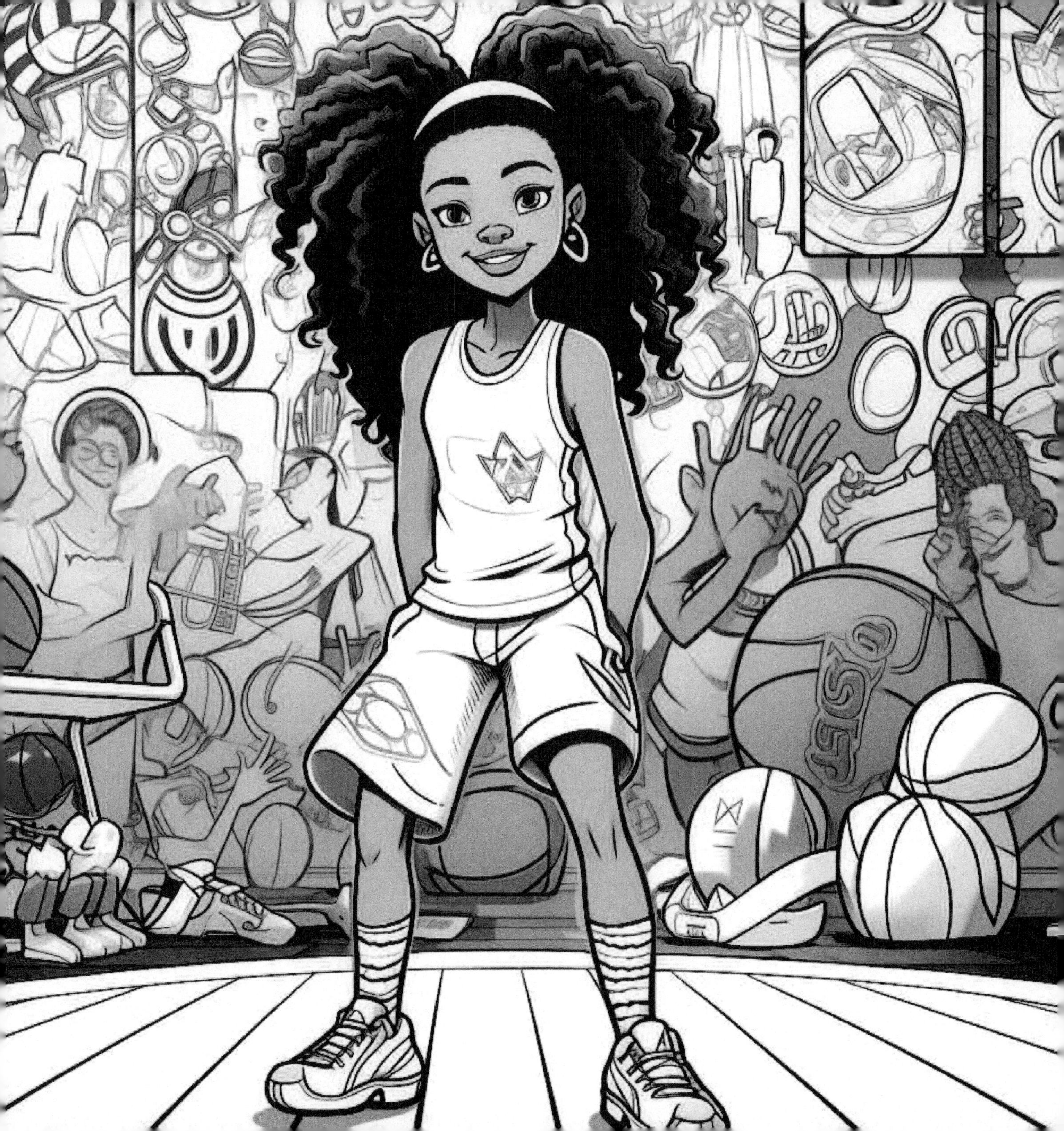

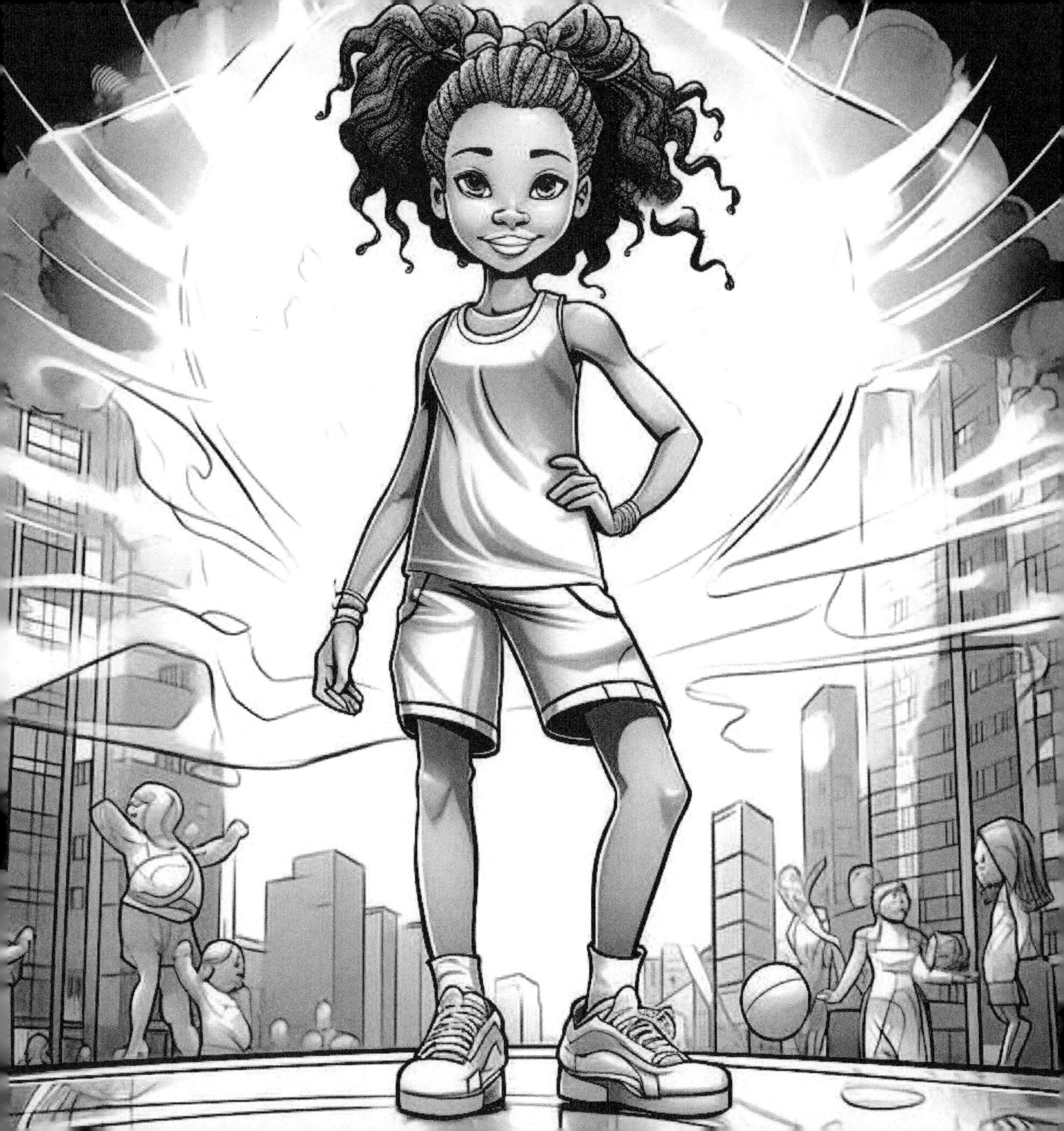

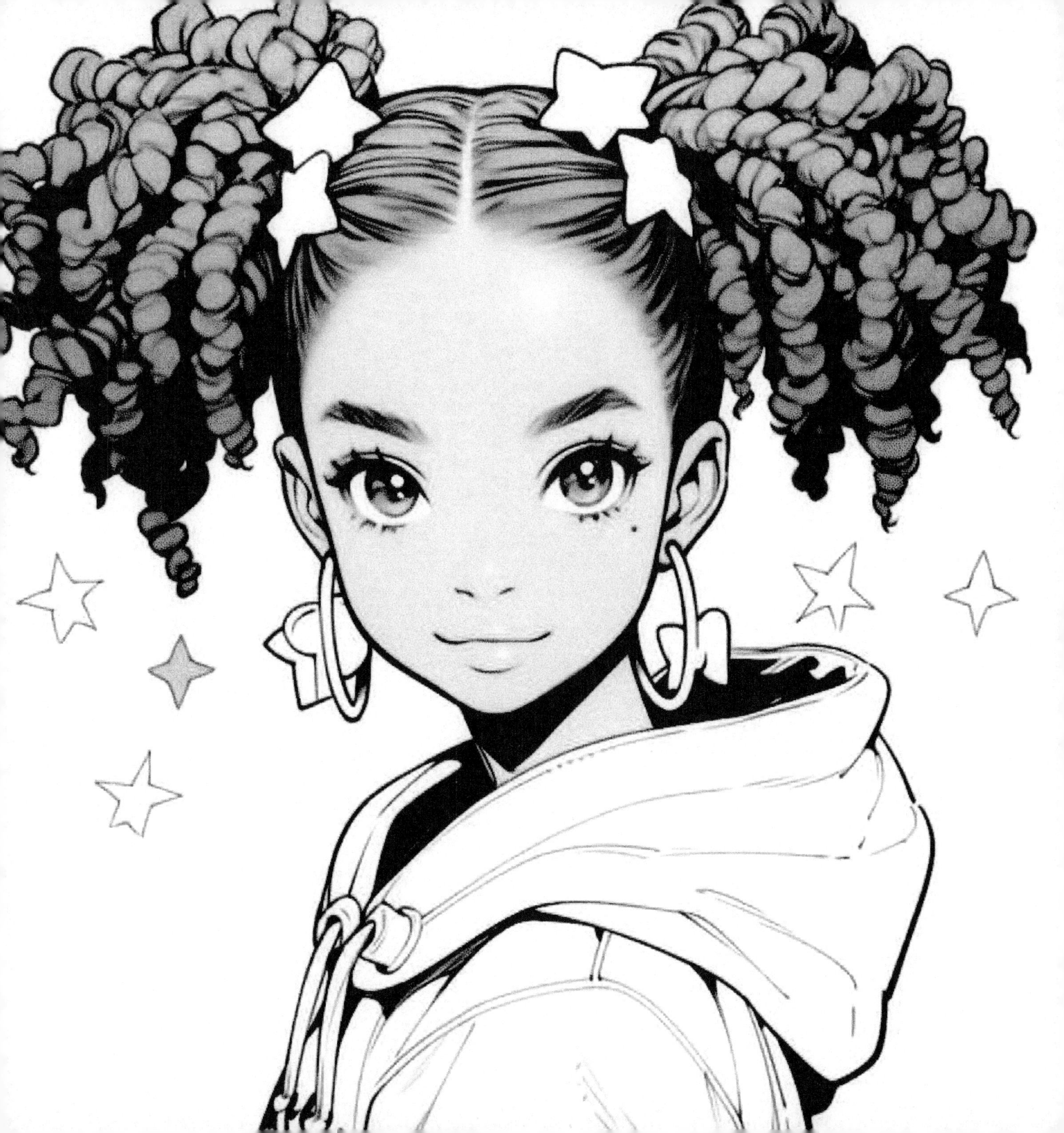

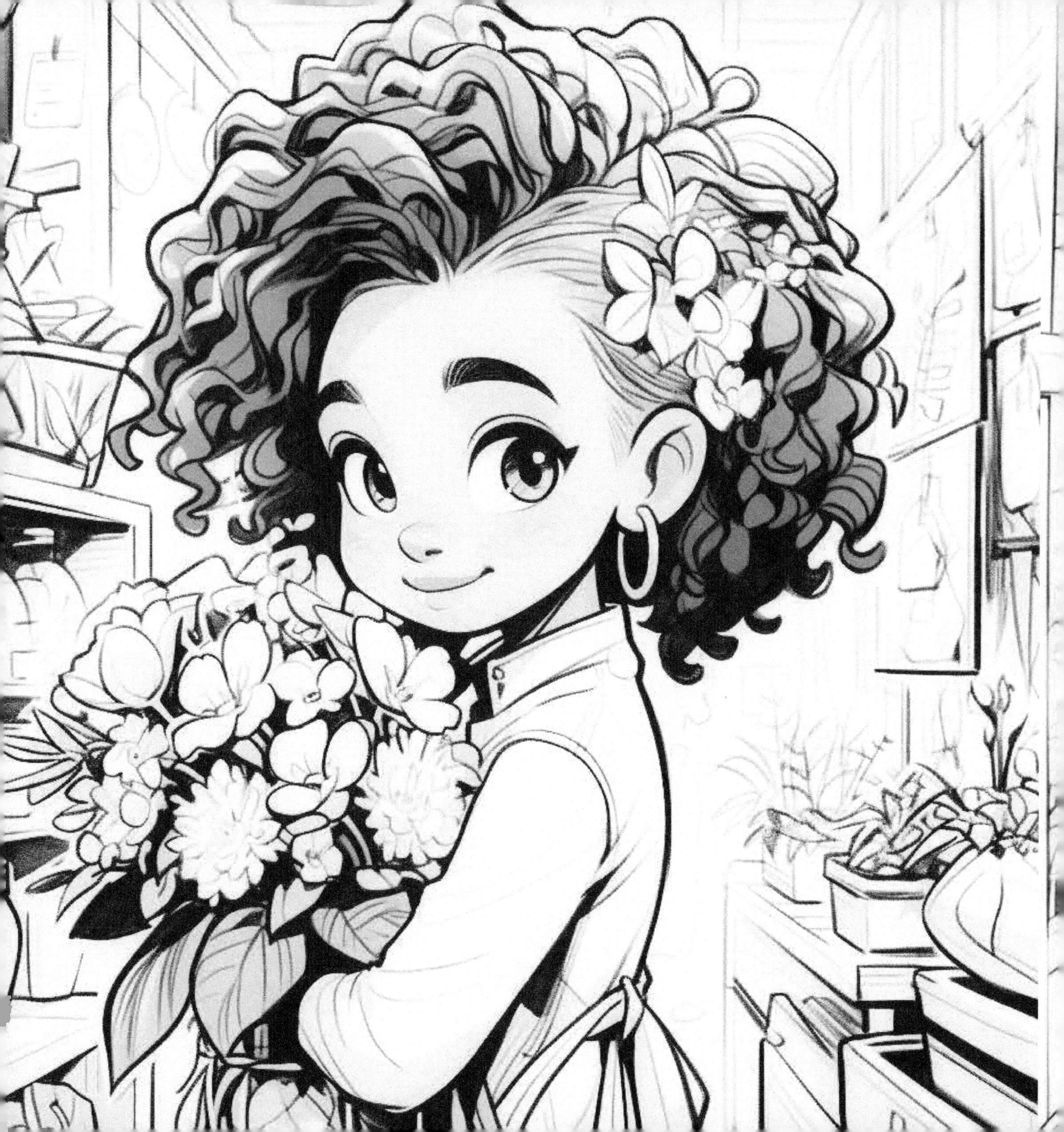

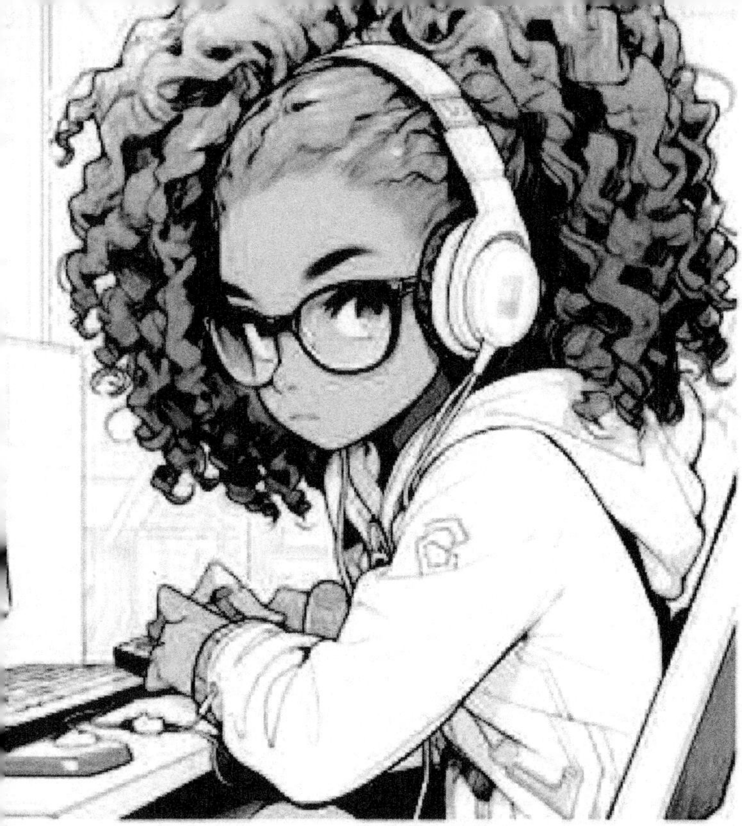
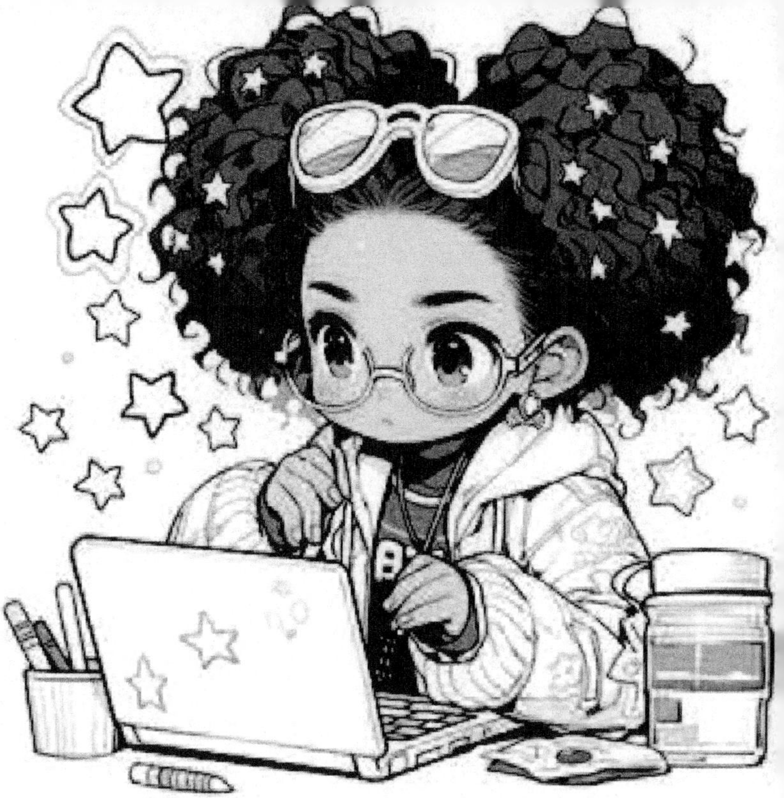
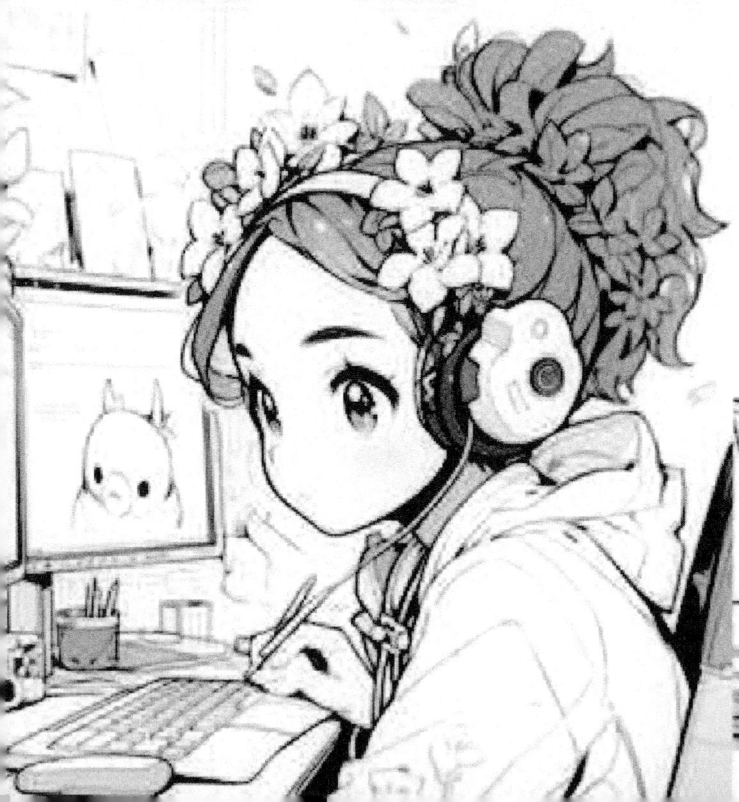
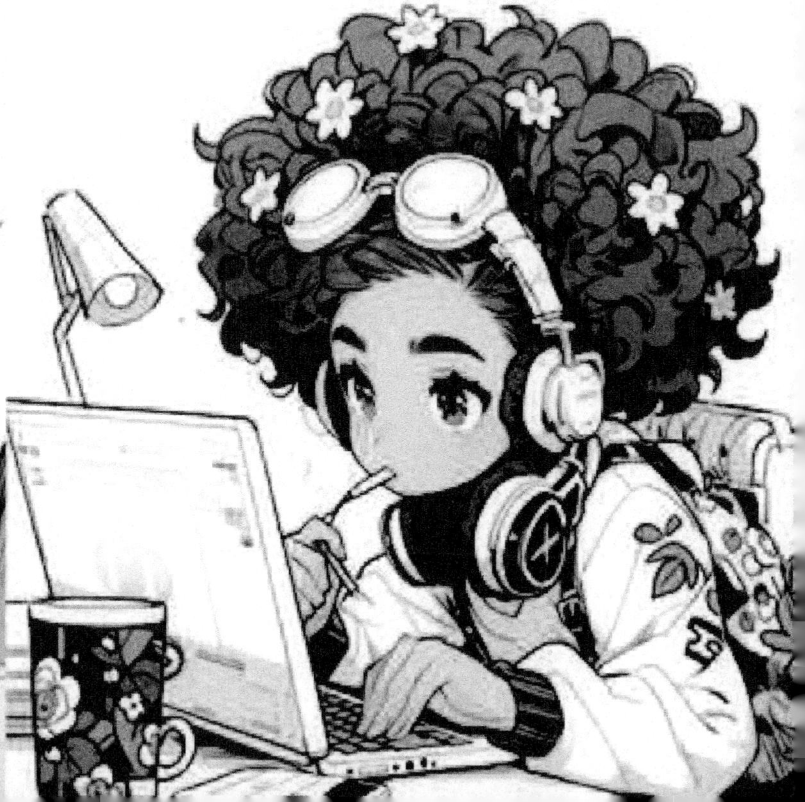

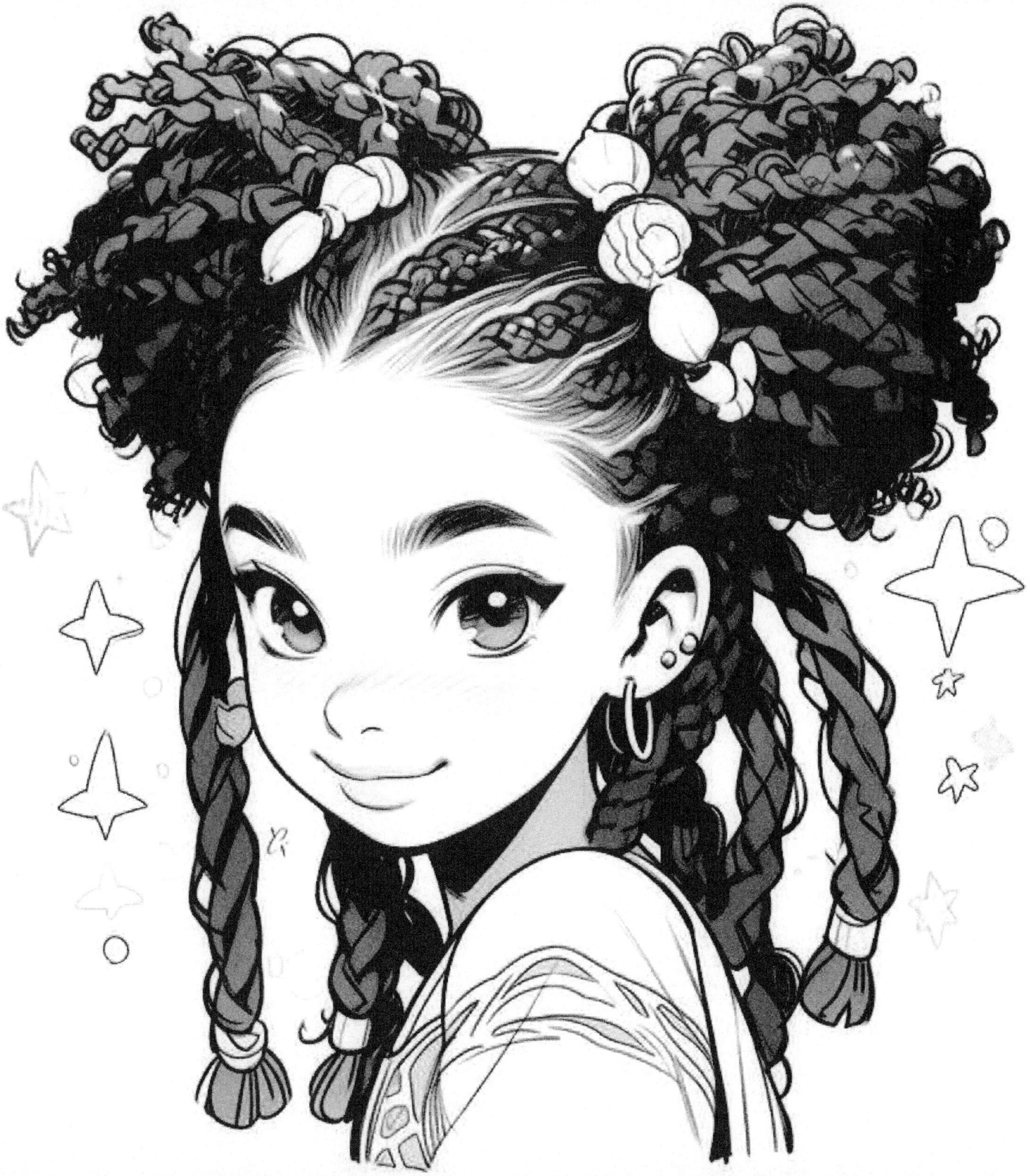

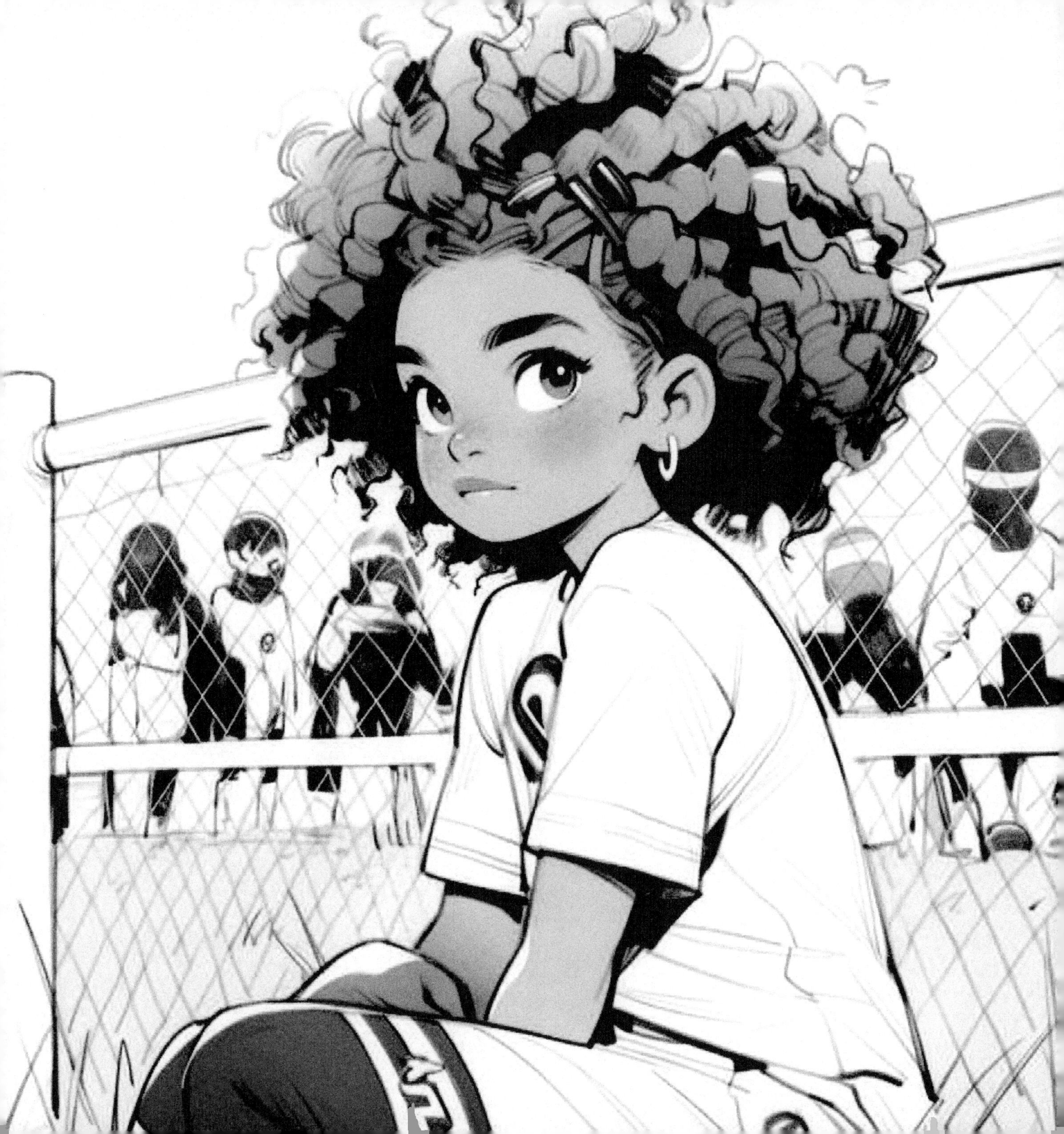

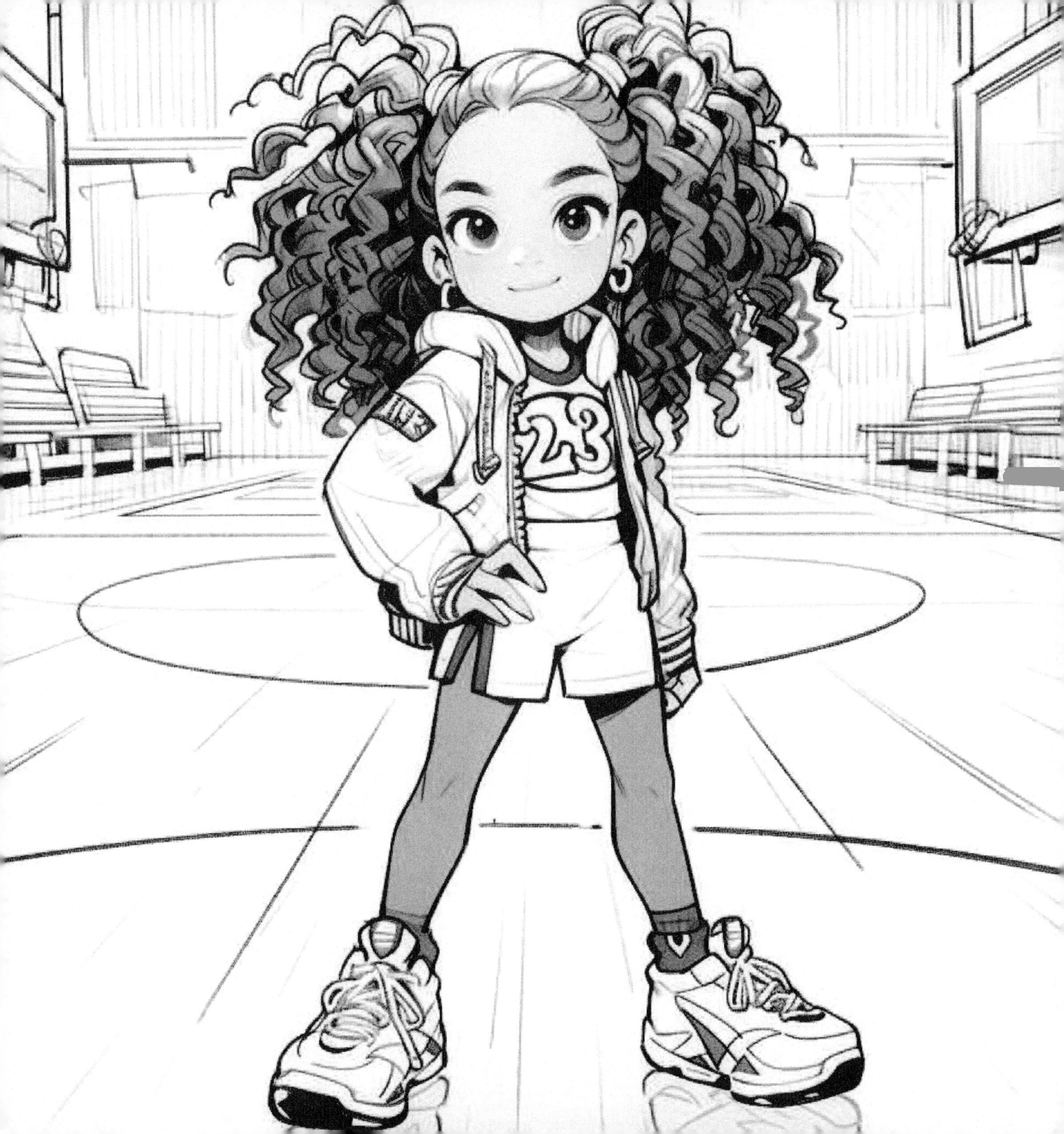
23

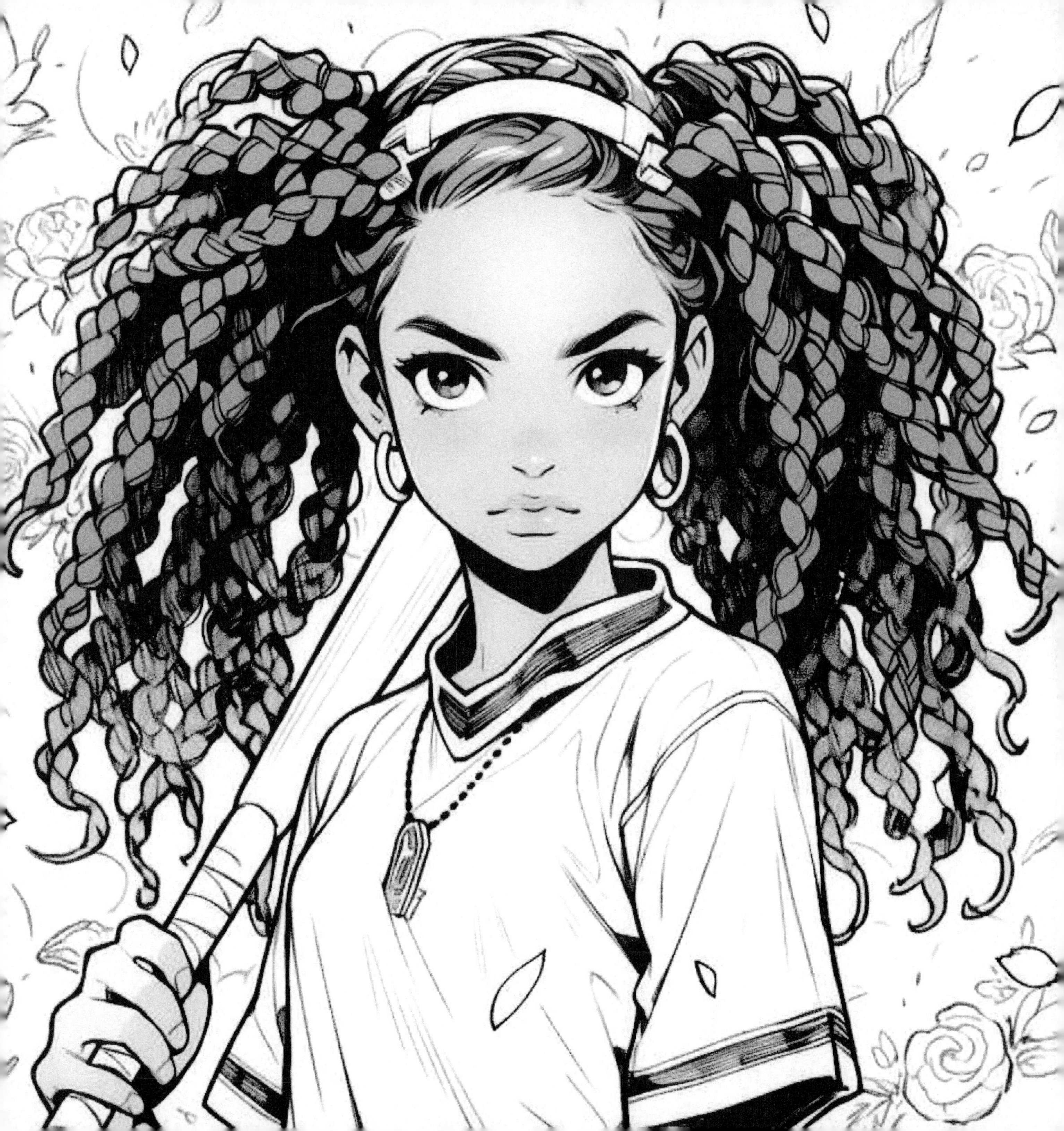

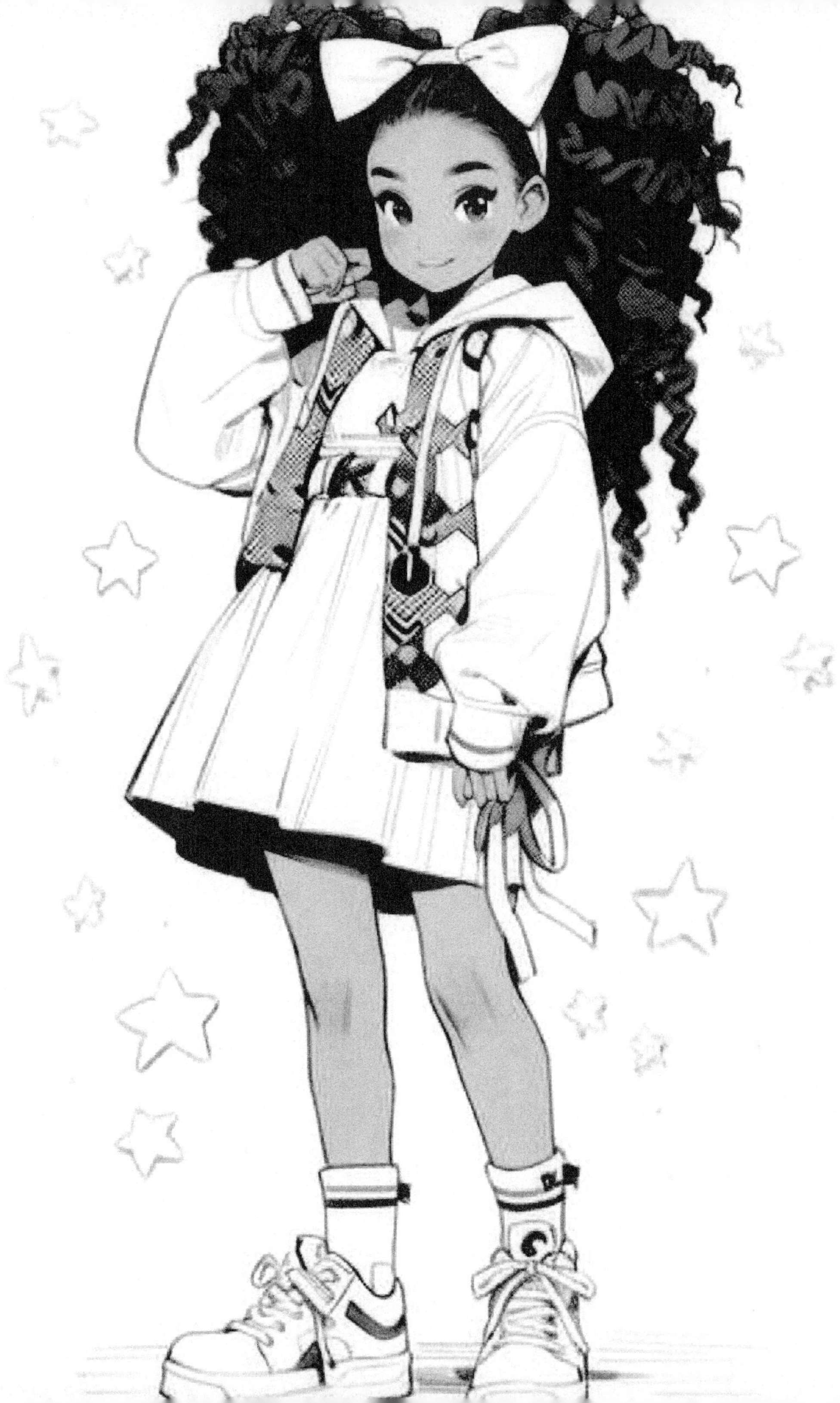

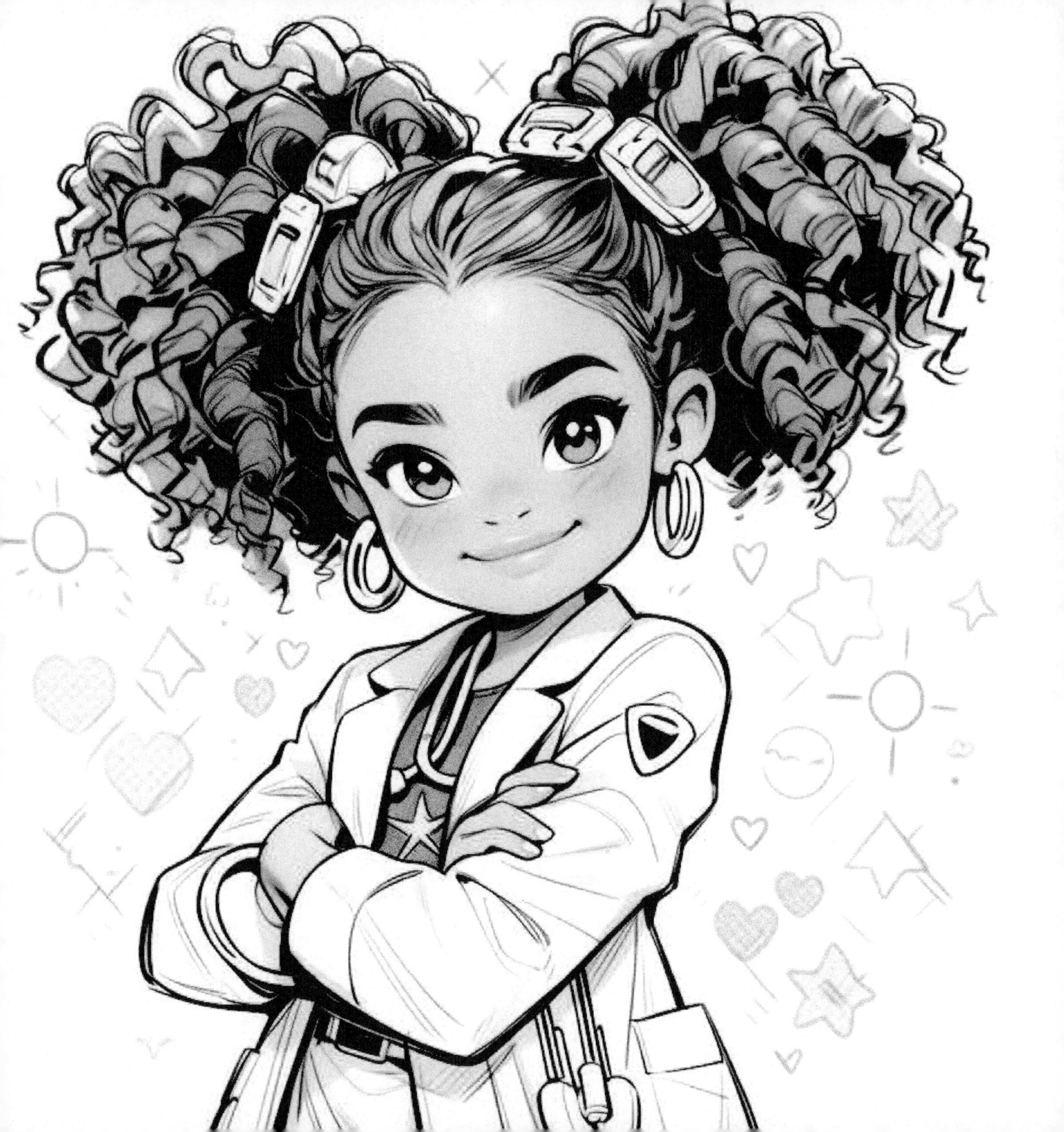

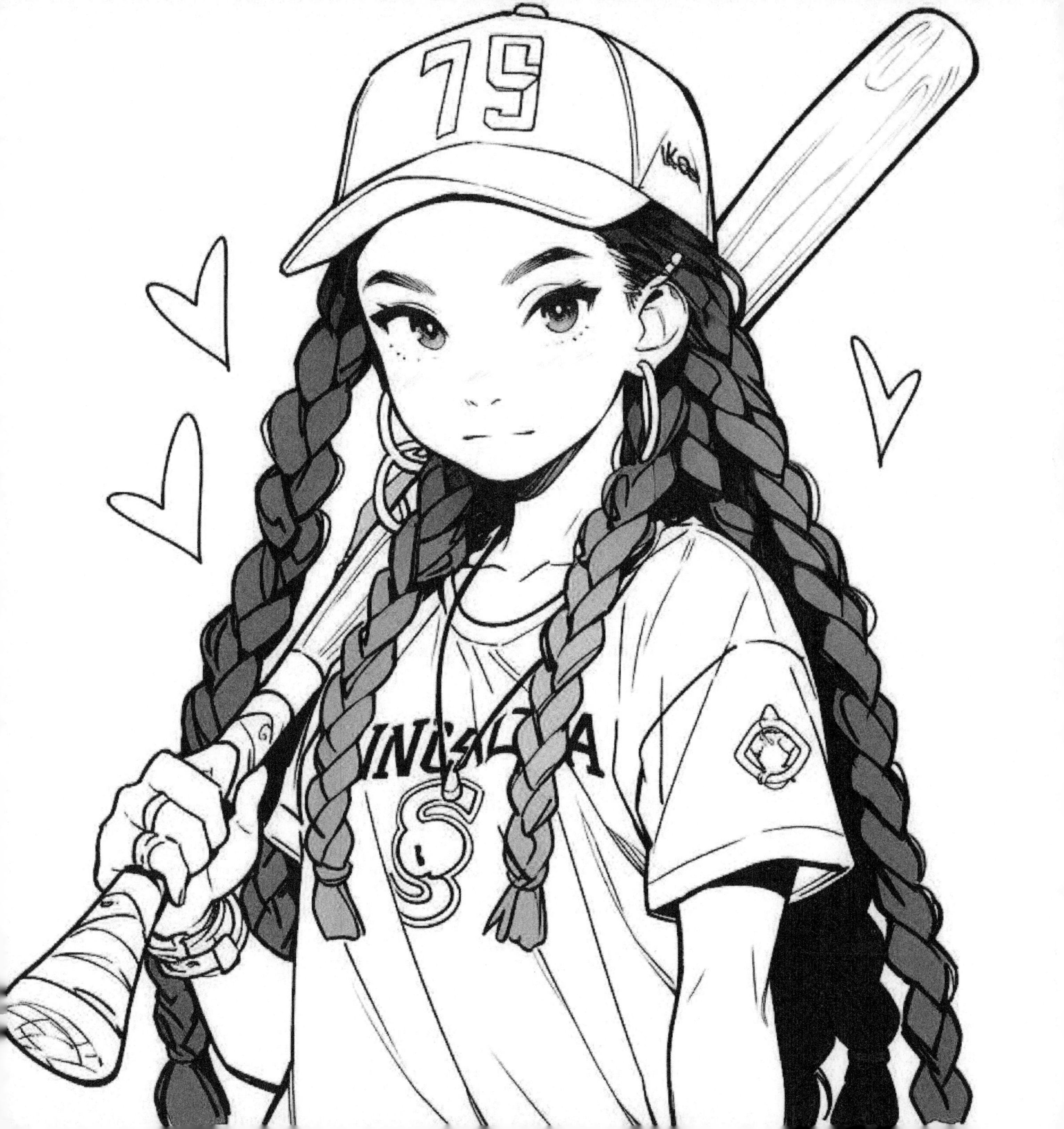
79

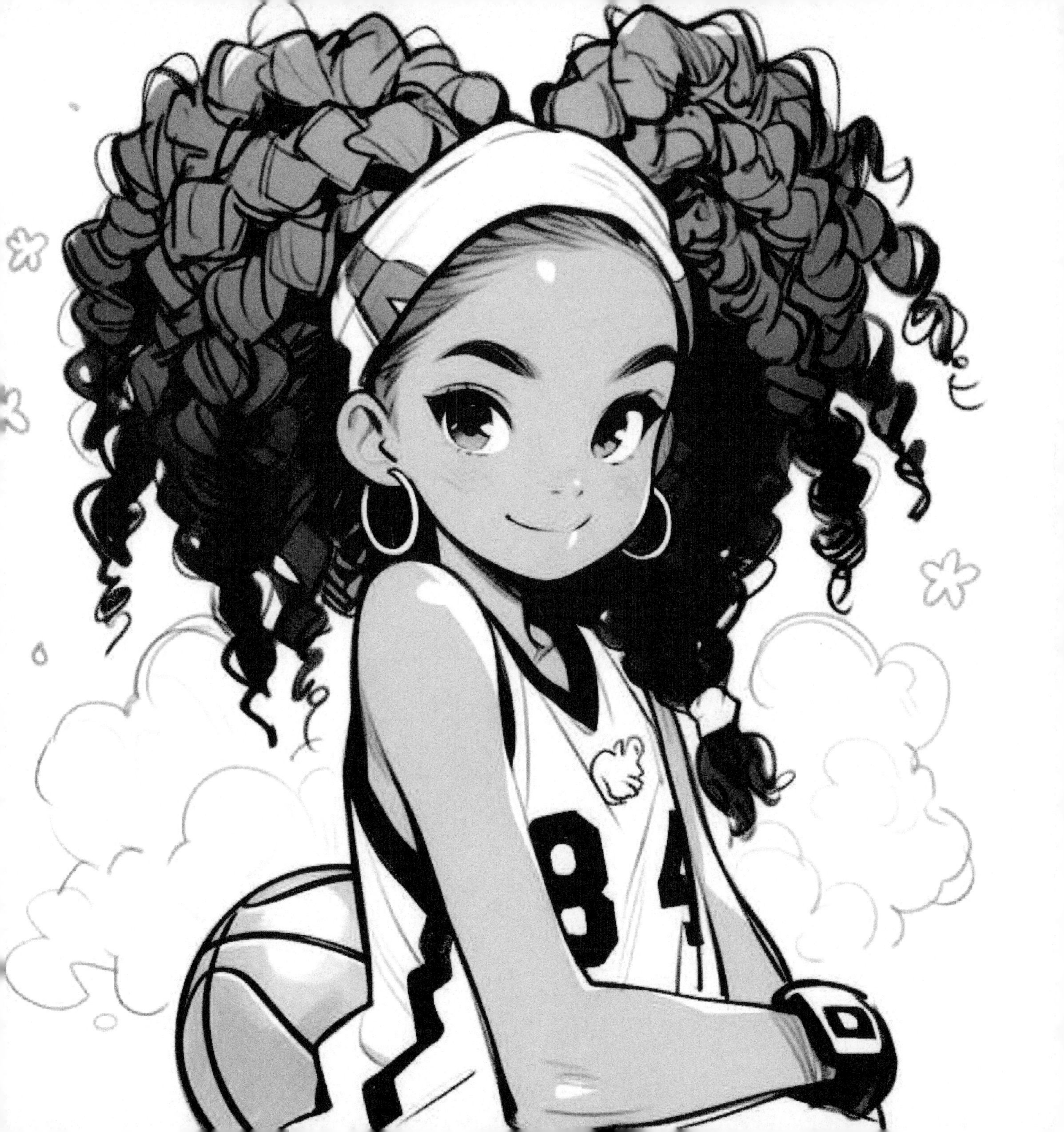
84

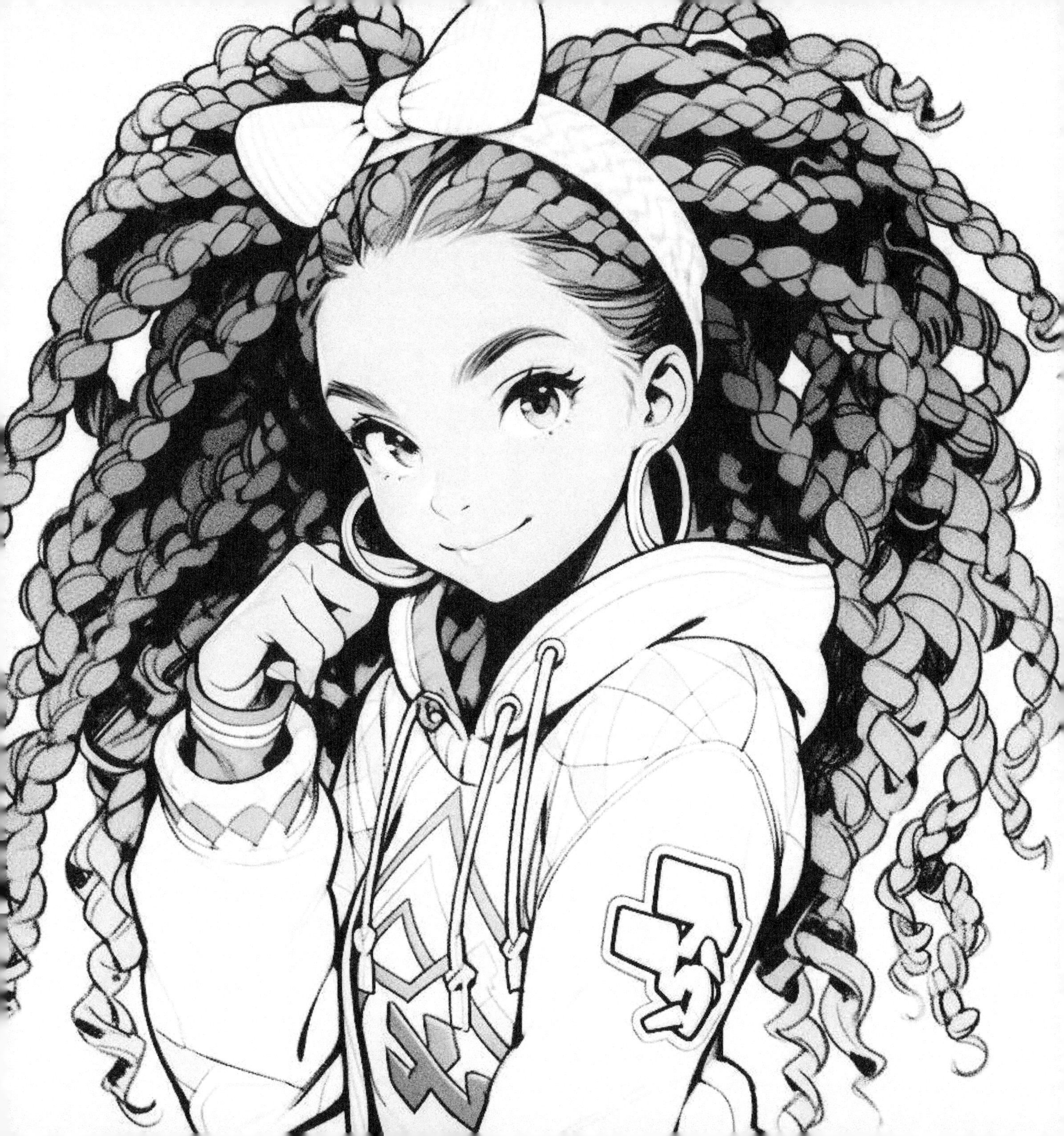

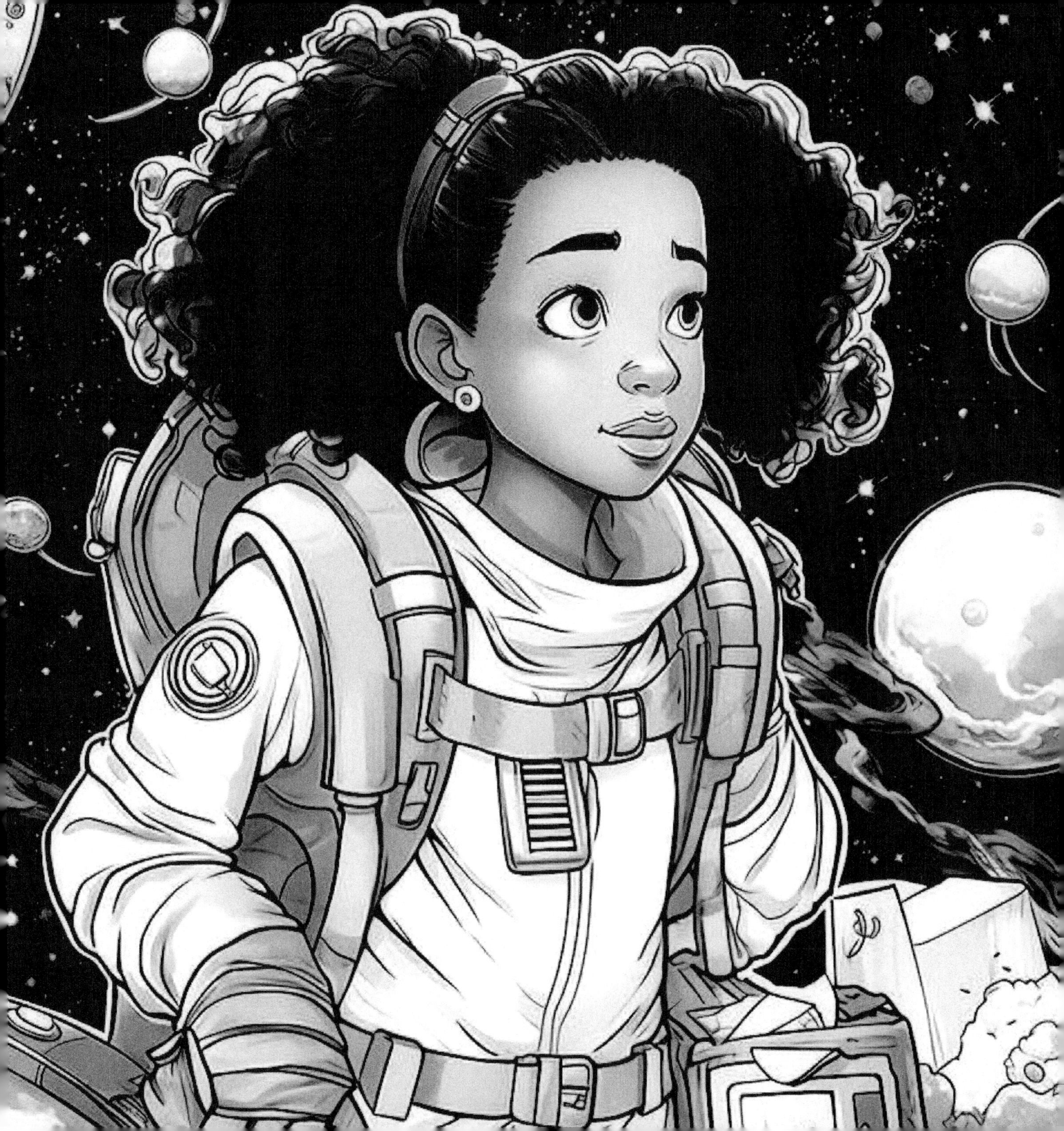

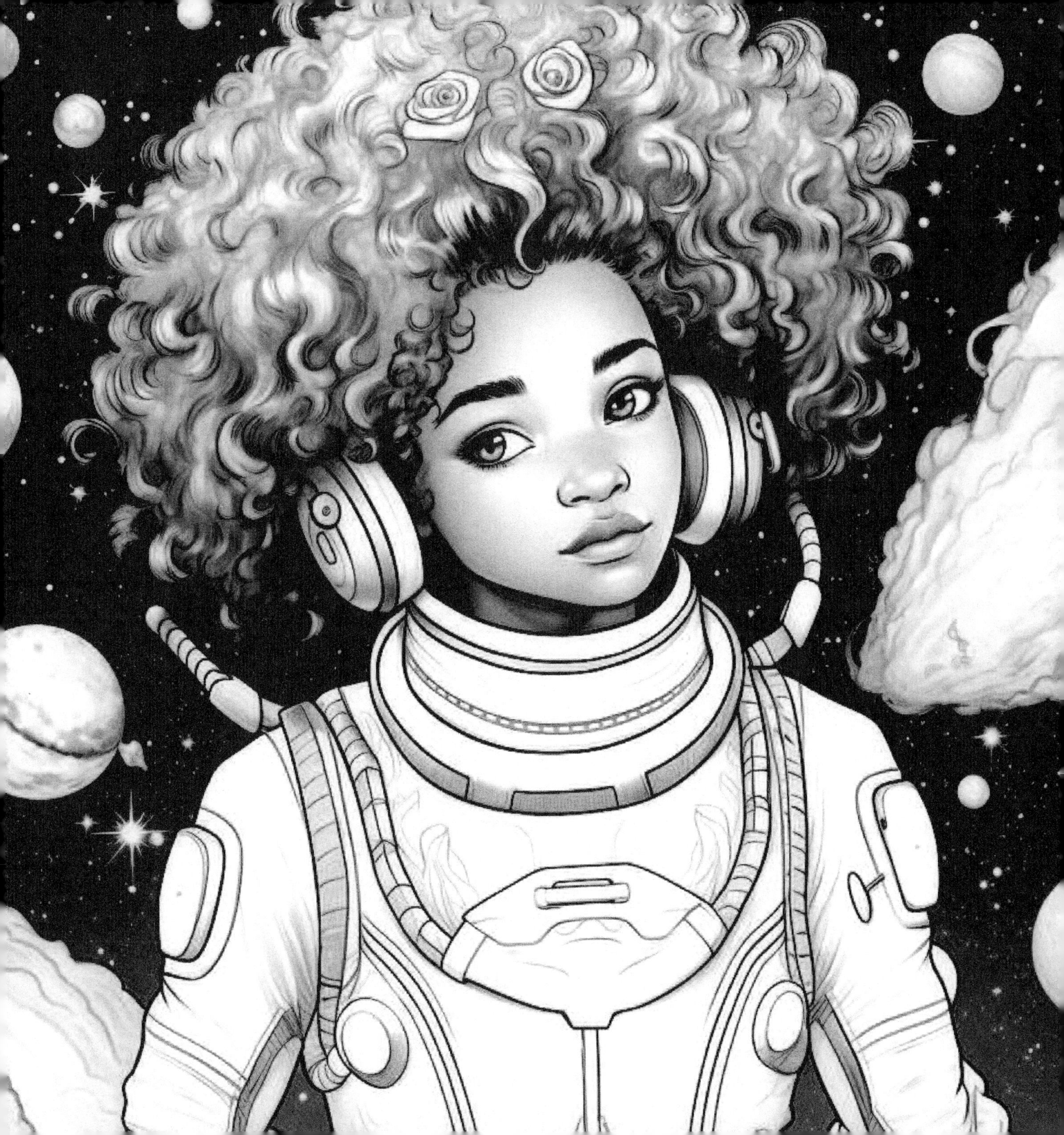

Printed in Great Britain
by Amazon

33107210R00057